Once Upon a Time . . .

The Proprietor

Ismail Merchant

BLOOMSBURY

First published in Great Britain in 1996

Screenplay copyright © Merchant Ivory Productions 1996

The making of the film copyright © Ismail Merchant 1996

All photographs copyright © Merchant Ivory Productions 1996

The moral right of the author has been asserted.

Bloomsbury Publishing Plc, 2 Soho Square, London, W1V 6HB.

A CIP catalogue record for this book is available from the British Library.

10 9 8 7 6 5 4 3 2 1

ISBN 0 7475 2905 1

Typeset by Hewer Text Composition Services, Edinburgh
Printed in England by Clays Ltd, St Ives Plc

The Proprietor

Contents

In memory of
my sister

Safia

List of colour illustrations

FOREWORD

I read once 'a smile can transform the World', this made me smile.

Throughout my life, I have experienced how a smile can be promising, soothing, even rewarding. Certain smiles have brought tears to my eyes.

The first time I met Ismail Merchant, he smiled as I crossed the threshold of the Indian Embassy in Paris. I noticed immediately the perfect rows of white teeth describing a harmonious curve called 'Angel wing'. I enjoyed instantly the warmth of his welcome, the energy of his voice. I was captivated. I still am.

From our initial encounter, a film was born and, I hope, a durable friendship. During the exhausting schedule of the filming of *The Proprietor* I saw again and again how powerful and mesmerizing Ismail's smile can be.

At times obstinate, impatient and unforgiving, he may scream at or threaten members of the crew and passers-by who delay or interrupt the filming of a scene. The victims stand still in terror, but when 'the shot is in the can' as we say, Ismail smiles. The grudge is forgotten, the storm is over.

Whoever has never seen Ismail reorganising the hectic traffic of taxis and tourist buses around Le Louvre museum and pyramid at 3 o'clock on a scorching, summer afternoon, cannot appreciate the magnitude of his overwhelming willpower and seduction. I am sure that bus and taxi drivers as well as policemen, who all surrendered to his orders, still remember the energetic Indian both cursing and smiling, who forced them to twist their rules and yield to his requests.

Steadfast in adversity, unpredictable, sweet and harsh, demanding and generous, Ismail is unforgettable. To me he means adventure, open doors and irresistible drive. Whenever something goes wrong, I live by one of his mottos: 'It's a blessing in disguise'.

Ismail's smile has transformed my life.

Jeanne Moreau
Paris, June 1996

ONCE UPON A TIME . . .

'ONLY CONNECT . . .'

When Jeanne Moreau heard that I was writing an account of how my film *The Proprietor* came into existence, she told me that the only way to begin the book was with the words 'Once upon a time' because it was so much like a fairy story. And she was right. It is a fairy story.

Most films come about because someone reads a book, a screenplay, or just a simple tale, and takes it from there. But never, in thirty-five years of film-making, has a film come to me out of the ether, from nowhere – unsought, unintended, unplanned. A film – not a book, or a story – demanding to be made.

Sometimes the gods send us gifts and we ignore them, failing to make the connection between those gifts and our own aspirations and endeavours. This is a story of what can happen when we don't ignore those gifts, when we allow ourselves to see the connections, and use them to heighten our own powers. 'Only connect . . .' – this is the epigraph of E.M. Forster's greatest novel, *Howards End*. Connect the opposites, connect the paths, connect with those apparently random gifts from the gods and the most extraordinary, unbelievable things can happen.

Or, in the words of Jeanne Moreau, 'Once upon a time . . .'

BEGINNINGS: PARIS, SPRING AND SUMMER 1994

Ever since we came to Paris in 1980 to make *Quartet* with Maggie Smith, Alan Bates and Isabelle Adjani, I kept hoping that some new project would materialize to take us back there. Like everyone else who has spent time in Paris I had, of course, fallen in love with the city, but there was another more compelling reason for wanting to work there again. The French take cinema seriously; it is as central to their culture as opera is to Italians or theatre to the British. In France film-makers are not seen as rogues and vagabonds but as artists, and they are treated with respect.

Unfortunately, with the exception of a week-long shoot in Paris during the making of our film *Mr and Mrs Bridge* in 1990, no French project was to surface for another fourteen years. Then, like buses and bills, they all came along at the same time. The first of these was *Jefferson in Paris*, a portrait of the American statesman and future president, Thomas Jefferson, during his time as ambassador to the court of King Louis XVI.

So, in the spring of 1994 the Merchant Ivory caravanserai returned to Paris, this time for an extended stay. We set up a production office for the film in rue Montmartre, in a part of an eighteenth-century building occupied by Humbert Balsan, my co-producer on *Quartet*, who would be working with us on our forthcoming French productions. Humbert began his career as an actor, and had just made the transition to producer with a documentary on Nadia Boulanger when we first met him in 1979. Since then he has produced more than thirty feature films.

For the present our home was a top-floor apartment on the Île St-Louis overlooking the Seine. But as we would be based in Paris for the foreseeable future, it occurred to me that it might be more practical and convenient to buy a place of our own rather than shift from one rented apartment to another. My partner and director James Ivory – cautious, circumspect Jim – warned me not to get involved in buying apartments in a country whose property laws I did not understand and whose language I barely spoke. In fact, he was very negative about the whole idea. So I immediately began to look at apartments.

In July 1994, during the shooting of *Jefferson*, another of our films, *In Custody*, was about to open in Paris. It was adapted from Anita Desai's novel dealing with the systematic destruction of the Urdu language and culture in India. This film had a special significance for me: as Urdu is my language and my culture, and therefore a subject very close to my heart, I had chosen to direct it myself – my first feature film as a director.

It starred Shashi Kapoor, one of India's most distinguished actors and one of my dearest friends. He had been in our very first film, *The Householder*, in 1962, and in a number of our subsequent films. Shashi was coming to Paris for the opening, and the Indian Ambassador, His Excellency Ranjit Sethi, and his charming wife Indu kindly offered to host a party in his honour. I was asked to submit my guest list and I included a few of the actors from *Jefferson*. Both Charlotte de Turckheim and Lambert Wilson, who were playing Marie Antoinette and Lafayette, come from theatre backgrounds, as does Shashi, so I thought it would be interesting for him to meet them.

Some instinct prompted me to invite, also, Jeanne Moreau. There was no logic in this, as we did not know each other and in fact had never even met. As an actress Moreau is in a league of her own, and I have been a great admirer of hers since 1962 when she completely captivated my heart with her performance in *Jules et Jim*. I followed up the Ambassador's invitation with a telephone call. Jeanne said she would like to come to the reception, but as she doesn't drive she asked if we could send a car for her, which I was happy to arrange. Until I came to know Jeanne I had no idea that in private life she is a very shy person: she has all the courage in the world in front of a camera or on stage, but social life is not something she greatly enjoys. Yet she accepted the invitation. Again there was no logical reason. As she told me later, she just felt she wanted to be there.

The Indian Embassy now occupies the grand mansion built for Lord Marlborough at the beginning of the nineteenth century.

This magnificently ornate building has had a distinguished history, but for all the great events that have unfolded under its gilded splendour the most important, for me at least, was that it was here I met Jeanne Moreau for the first time.

She arrived, as luminous and transfixing in the flesh as on the screen. I introduced myself, then introduced her to Shashi whom, in fact, she had already met in 1985 when she served as the President of the Jury at the New Delhi Film Festival at which Shashi was a guest. As soon as we met I felt an odd sensation that I had known Jeanne all my life. Of course this often happens when you meet famous people for the first time: you already know them, in a way, from their work, from newspaper articles and television interviews. And although there was an element of this in our first meeting, the familiarity I felt went beyond that. There was none of that awkwardness of making conversation with someone you don't know, of trying to find something to say, of feigning interest in what they are saying. I felt an immediate rapport with Jeanne that I still can't explain – it was almost a spiritual connection. Much later, I learned from Jeanne that she felt exactly the same way on meeting me.

During our conversation I told her about my film *In Custody* and invited her to the première. Regrettably, she realized she would be away from Paris then, but we arranged to see it together on her return. When we parted that evening I had no idea how this brief meeting would transform my life over the next twelve months. Looking back now, it seems that Jeanne Moreau and I were not destined to meet until that time, in that place and in those particular circumstances. Our paths had come so close to crossing on three previous occasions that it seems as if the fates had conspired to prevent it until that moment.

The first occasion was in 1985 when we were in Florence shooting *A Room with a View*. Florence is a small city and we had appropriated much of it for the film, including the main square, Piazza Signoria. There was simply no way of avoiding us. In addition, some of the unit, including Jim and myself, were staying at the Hotel Excelsior. Jeanne was in Florence at the same time, giving master-classes at Vittorio Gassman's theatre school,

6

and she too was staying at the Excelsior until the noise (ours, probably) drove her to seek quieter accommodation. She was completely unaware that we were shooting the film and we had no idea of her presence in the city either.

Some years later Jeanne came on a visit to New York, and her friend the photo-journalist Mark Ginsberg, who contributes to such magazines as *Vanity Fair*, *Cosmopolitan* and *Interview* and who is also a friend of ours, took her on a drive to the Hudson Valley. When Mark realized they were only a few miles from our house in upstate New York he decided to call in and see us. They met Jim, the writer Ruth Prawer Jhabvala (the essential third member of the Merchant Ivory team) and her husband Jhab. I was absent at the time and later, when I heard about the wonderful dinner they all had together, I was deeply disappointed that I had missed meeting Jeanne Moreau.

More recently, when Jim was in Paris casting *Jefferson*, he called Jeanne and arranged to meet her. He was considering her for a part in that film, but Jeanne misunderstood the nature of his call, believing it to be social rather than business. So when they began to discuss work and Jeanne told Jim she was currently preoccupied with writing, Jim didn't pursue the matter, presuming that she was too busy. I had no idea of Jim's plan until after this meeting and, once again, I had missed the chance of meeting Jeanne Moreau.

Between that first meeting with Jeanne at the Indian Embassy and her return to Paris, our search for an apartment continued. Sometimes Marc Tissot, a young Swiss actor who speaks good English, accompanied me as interpreter because my French was still rather rudimentary. I had met Marc on the recommendation of the eminent film critic and author David Robinson, whom we have known for thirty years. David is one of the few genuine authorities on cinema, with a knowledge, understanding and affection for his subject all too rare in these days of glib and shallow journalism. Chief among his many books is the definitive biography of Charlie Chaplin (when Richard Attenborough came to make the film of Chaplin's life he asked David to collaborate with him on the screenplay).

Marc Tissot came to see me in London just as I was about to leave for India where *In Custody* was to be shown at the Calcutta Film Festival. As usual, I was very short of time: I made polite – if hurried – conversation, offered him tea, took his phone number to give to our casting director in Paris, then headed off to the other side of the world.

I felt bad that I hadn't been able to give Marc more time. On my return to Paris I called him in Geneva to see whether he had met the casting director and Jim, and was pleased to hear that he had been offered a small part in *Jefferson*. Some weeks later Marc was in Paris and called at the rue Montmartre office; he wanted to check the dates of filming because he was about to do a play in Lausanne.

To make up for our abrupt earlier meeting I invited him to dinner. He talked with great feeling about acting, and told me how much he admired Jeanne Moreau and longed for an opportunity to work with her. I am always drawn to people who feel passionately about their work, and Marc's intense commitment, as well as his Hollywood matinée idol looks, suggested that this was an actor who deserved to be given a chance. I went to see his play in Lausanne, saw him act in *Jefferson*, and earmarked him for some unspecified future project – unaware then that his presence would feature so prominently in my more immediate plans.

It was from Marc that I heard a fascinating story concerning an acclaimed French writer who owned a number of *chambres de bonne* (the servants' rooms in the attics of old buildings) and rented them out, usually to people without official papers, illegal immigrants, people with no rights. This was not done from a sense of philanthropy, however. Each month she would take a large basket and go from room to room all over Paris demanding her rents. If the tenants were unable to pay, this author of sensitive works on the human condition simply kicked them out. Later, when I discussed this story with some friends, I was also told that this writer kept a string of lovers in these rooms and had some incredible affairs.

I was haunted by these stories, this strange double life: the discrepancy between the public and private faces of a person. It gradually occurred to me that Jeanne could play the part of a writer extremely well – few actors have the ability to convey an inner life with such conviction. I wasn't interested in making a bio-pic of the French writer Marc had told me about, but an insubstantial thought had planted itself in my mind, and I had no idea how it might develop.

Jeanne returned to Paris and we re-confirmed our arrangement to see *In Custody*. I was detained on the set of *Jefferson* that evening and arrived late at the cinema. The friends I had asked to join us were there – but no sign of Jeanne. Had she left, offended at being kept waiting? The box office clerk told me that Miss Moreau had collected her ticket and gone into the auditorium. I eventually found her sitting in the middle row. The film was about to start so – except to apologize – there was no time to chat. When it was over, however, Jeanne turned to me with tears in her eyes and embraced me.

We left the cinema and the four of us went to a nearby Chinese restaurant where we were joined by Marc. Although I was the only connection between the individual parties, everyone chatted like old friends. All through dinner Jeanne talked about the film. These were not the hollow compliments you feel obliged to pay a director whose film you've watched in his presence: I felt the genuine emotion behind her words.

I mentioned to Jeanne that I had an idea for a film I wanted to direct. At present it was nothing more than that, I explained. But if it could ever be developed into something – might she consider looking at it? There was no question about it, Jeanne replied. We both felt we were destined to work together.

When the filming of *Jefferson* was completed in July 1994 I returned to New York. I began to give some thought to devel-oping the idea for the new film. Normally I would have gone straight to Ruth, but I knew that she was very much involved with the script for our forthcoming film on Pablo Picasso.

Earlier that summer I had met the French playwright Jean-

9

Marie Besset at a party given by the French Cultural Attaché in New York, and back in Paris I had seen his current play, *Ce qui arrive et ce qu'on attend*. Besset divides his time between Paris and New York, and it occurred to me that he might be the right person to work with on this screenplay. We met to discuss the possibility and he seemed very keen. Beyond wanting to cast Jeanne in the part of a writer, and a few other loose ideas, however, there was no story or plot as yet.

The first scenario Besset suggested was set in the theatre world. Jeanne's part was that of a woman who has a theatre company and is involved in some kind of tug-of-war with another theatre company and that didn't interest me at all. We had covered similar ground with *Jane Austen in Manhattan* in 1980. In this film we had used fragments of Jane Austen's only play as the basis for a story in which rival New York theatre companies compete for this material. Now I wanted to do something completely new. Besset had not taken up my idea of the writer as the central character, so we returned to that theme. Besset came back with something interesting, but it was still not quite right.

While Besset continued working on the screenplay I flew back to Paris and, because the lease on our Île St-Louis apartment was soon to expire, redoubled my efforts to find something to buy.

THE APARTMENT

Marc and I called a number of estate agents and contacted many friends who might know of something interesting that was for sale. We must have seen over twenty apartments, including a beautiful one in the Marais which was too expensive for us to consider, before someone suggested a place on Avenue Foch. This had been repossessed by the bank and was being put up for auction. I had never been to a French property auction before and wanted to familiarize myself with the procedure before the auction of the Avenue Foch apartment. So I went along to one as a spectator, and was fascinated by the traditional ritual, which involves three candles, lit at different stages of the bidding, and the presence of magistrates. It struck me as a wonderful scene for a film.

However, the Avenue Foch apartment was eventually withdrawn from auction because the bankers saw the possibility of a deal, and they invited us to make a direct offer. Unfortunately, an Italian buyer offered 50,000 francs more, so we lost it. Almost immediately we found another place on Avenue President Kennedy, just opposite the Eiffel Tower. This apartment had once belonged to Pamela Harriman, the American Ambassador to Paris. Again I made an offer, but the three sisters involved in selling the property began to squabble amongst themselves, and somehow in the midst of all this the apartment was never sold.

Of the dozens of apartments I had seen, these had been the only two that I had liked and could afford, and I was a little disappointed that I hadn't been able to buy either. But I believe that when you fail to get something you want, it's because you are not meant to have it – that there is something better waiting for you.

In order to simplify our lives while we worked in France, as well as to comply with French bureaucracy and qualify for the subsidies available to French-based film-makers, I decided that we should establish a permanent office in Paris. And so, in August 1994,

Merchant Ivory France was born. My niece Rahila Bootwala, who has lived in France for some years and speaks fluent French, English and Hindi, was put in charge together with Marc Tissot.

While we had sub-let office space from Humbert Balsan during *Jefferson* we had become familiar with the area around rue Montmartre and wanted to remain there. In Humbert's building there was a large space where we had lodged the art department for *Jefferson* and which was now vacant. In its present state, however, it was uninhabitable; it resembled a bomb site, with huge naked eighteenth-century beams perilously attached to the rafters. The office needed to be ready by September, so I asked Marc to find some good builders who could begin work as soon as possible. This presented a problem – August is the month when the French traditionally take their annual vacation, and nothing is done during this time.

A few of the contractors who were still working in August agreed to come and see the place, but either they were too expensive for us or else they felt it wasn't possible to complete the work in the given time. We had noticed some of the shops in rue Montmartre were in the process of being redecorated and decided to approach the builders working in one of these shops. The man in charge of this particular renovation was Angelo Manzolini, an Italian who had worked for many years with the distinguished French designer Philippe Starck, and Marc negotiated a deal with him. Angelo came and saw the space, accepted our limitations of money and time, and by the end of September had created an efficient working office for us.

During this period Angelo learned of our interest in finding an apartment and suggested a place he knew, in an eighteenth-century *hôtel particulier* (a large private town house) in the Saint Germain district. He made arrangements with the estate agent for Marc and me to see it. We were told that the place had been unoccupied since the death of the owner some three years earlier, and we expected to find a cold, bare, barren place. So we were surprised when the door was opened by a butler, Mamadu, a tiny black man wearing the traditional butler's red and black striped waistcoat, his disapproval of our visit evident in his expression.

The place was still furnished – over-furnished, one might say – and in a rather eccentric way with an odd yet compatible mix of English and French antiques. We were led into the dining room where a large table was set with delicate porcelain and crystal, as though ready to receive a dinner party. The walls throughout the apartment were hung with a collection of paintings including a number of Soutines.

As we went from room to room it became increasingly impossible to take in all the detail; so many styles, so many objects, so much colour. No corner had been overlooked – even the walls of the tiny, narrow corridor leading to the kitchen had elaborate Chinese murals framed by gilded bamboo. There was simply no word to describe the style of this extraordinary place. It was just too eclectic, too idiosyncratic, too personal. And beyond the antiques and the objects were the tiny details of someone's life; the hairbrush in the bedroom, the collapsed pack of cards on a card table in the drawing room. Everything left, perhaps, just as it was three years ago, as though the occupant would return. And Mamadu, suspicious of our interest in this place, a silent shadow in our footsteps.

Marc suggested that it would make an excellent setting for the film we had in mind – its distinctive ambience particularly suited the character of a writer. I agreed with him, and we looked at the apartment again from this other perspective.

When the estate agent asked if I was interested I didn't hesitate. I told her I wanted it. But when she asked me to make an offer, I had absolutely no idea – I had seen so many apartments in recent months that I had some idea of property values in Paris, but how could one put a price on a place like this? It was evident that it would need quite a bit of work – the wiring, plumbing and heating all required attention – and I had no idea if the building was in good shape structurally, but I wasn't going to let this apartment slip through my fingers, so I made an offer. The agent said she thought the vendor would expect more, but she would convey the offer to him.

I felt that this apartment, once restored and refurnished, would suit me and that I could live there very comfortably and make the place my own – and an added bonus was that we could make it an important location for our film.

The next morning all my plans collapsed when the estate agent phoned Marc and told him that the vendor had rejected the offer. In fact he had been insulted by it. Apparently he was under the impression that I was some big-shot Hollywood producer, a philistine who wanted to buy up Paris for next to nothing. By now, however, I felt so strongly that this apartment and the film were somehow connected that I couldn't just let it go. I suggested to Marc that we should increase the offer, but the agent told him there was no point – the vendor would never sell us the apartment and didn't want to hear from us again.

By another of those strange coincidences that feature so strongly in this story, Véronique de Goldschmidt, a friend of ours who not only acts as a photographers' representative but also deals in the very grand end of real estate and knew we were looking for an apartment, sent Marc a gift of a book called *Parisian Interiors*, which Marc showed to me. It included a section on the apartment we had just seen. Intrigued, I read the text and it all began to make sense.

This had been the home of Madeleine Castaing, the doyenne of French interior design and decoration, and one of the best-known figures in Paris, who had numbered many great artists, writers and musicians amongst her circle of friends. She had died the day before her ninety-eighth birthday, still a style-setter, and her business was now controlled by her son Michel Castaing – the man who wanted nothing to do with us.

Despite this set-back, I wanted to show Jeanne the apartment to see how she felt about the place as a location for her character in the film. Marc called the agent to say that Jeanne Moreau was interested in looking at the place. Until that time, Jeanne had no idea how seriously I had taken the initial suggestion that we should work together, that I had already commissioned a screen-play for her. I telephoned her: 'Jeanne, we are sending a car for you to take you to see *your* apartment'. I put the phone down before she could ask any questions.

Once again the agent was waiting for us by the entrance of the building and took us up. Jeanne looked around the foyer and walked into the dining room. As she took it in, she slowly sat down at the table. All the handles of the coffee cups were pointing in the same direction – except one. Jeanne reached out and delicately turned the cup so that its handle was symmetrical with the others. It seemed as though she was already in character.

Jeanne got up and we followed her into the other rooms. In Madeleine Castaing's bedroom Jeanne touched my arm and I looked at her and followed her gaze to the ceiling. It was extraordinary – the whole ceiling was a vast painting of fat pink cherubs sitting on fluffy white clouds against a misty pink and grey sky. I hadn't noticed it before – but then it was impossible to take everything in on a first visit, or even a second. There would be constant surprises in this place.

We left the apartment and I took Jeanne to show her Madeleine Castaing's shop on the ground floor. The window was full of Castaing's letters, and photographs of her with friends such as Cocteau and Horowitz. We didn't go inside – which was just as well because, unknown to us, Michel Castaing was there at the time and saw us staring at the window.

Later Jeanne, Marc and I had dinner at the Café des Beaux Arts. Jeanne's response to the place was the same as Marc's and mine had been – that it was special and right. Then she told us that she'd had the most extraordinary feeling when she entered the apartment, a sense that she knew the place and that everything in it was familiar to her. She seemed a little disturbed by this. Days later she realized that she had actually visited the apartment before: Jean Cocteau had taken her to a dinner party there, and Madeleine Castaing had been her hostess.

I knew we had to get the apartment. But the following day I was due to leave for New York for script consultations with Jean-Marie Besset. In the light of recent developments, I also had to try to find a way of making the apartment the catalyst of our story. So before I left Paris I gave Marc a small task to perform – I asked him to acquire the apartment for us.

When Michel Castaing had seen us outside the shop, he had naturally recognized Jeanne and assumed that I was the philistine

Hollywood film producer. The next day the estate agent called Marc and told him how enraged Michel Castaing had been by the visit, that he was convinced we didn't really want the apartment except to shoot a movie there. Castaing's answer was no – and that was final.

Marc could see that he would get nowhere with the estate agent, so he decided to go to the shop and make contact personally. The shop is run by Madame Lombardini who trained with Madeleine Castaing and continues her work. Marc entered and introduced himself, but Madame Lombardini ignored him completely and just carried on with her work as though he were invisible. Marc sat there until she finally looked at him and demanded to know why he had come. Marc explained that there had been a misunderstanding, that we *did* want to use the apartment for a film because we felt there should be a record of this extraordinary place, but the primary reason for buying it was that I intended to live there.

Marc pointed out, very logically, that we had been able to recreate eighteenth-century Paris for *Jefferson*, and, if necessary, we could just as easily create an apartment identical to Madeleine Castaing's. If Madame Lombardini had ever seen our films or knew anything at all about Merchant Ivory, continued Marc, then she would realize that we are in the business of preserving things rather than destroying them. All he wanted, he said finally, was a chance to put his case to Monsieur Castaing, and if he couldn't convince Monsieur Castaing of the sincerity of our intentions then we wouldn't bother him again.

Madame Lombardini said nothing, but she picked up the phone and called Michel Castaing at his office. She told him that she thought he should come to the shop and hear what Marc had to say. Monsieur Castaing refused at first, but Madame Lombardini pleaded and he reluctantly agreed to come.

Fifteen minutes later Michel Castaing arrived and Madame Lombardini introduced him to Marc. They went upstairs to a small room above the shop, and Monsieur Castaing listened as Marc explained our motives for wanting to make a film in his mother's apartment, how much we loved the place, and that as far as possible we wanted to keep it as it was. Then Marc listened open-mouthed as Monsieur Castaing told him about the kind of buyers he had seen – Americans who wanted to tear down the bedroom ceiling and the Chinese corridor, turn the exquisite drawing room into a kitchen, and put a jacuzzi in the Empire bathroom. Marc protested that we wanted to keep all the architectural details exactly as they were, since those were what we were buying the apartment *for*. We even wanted to keep some of the furniture if he would agree to sell it. They talked for a long time, and Marc heard the curious and touching history of the apartment.

Madeleine Castaing had bought it in 1960, then spent six years preparing it down to the last detail. Furniture, objects, porcelain had to be exactly right – even the textiles and fabrics for the upholstery and curtains had been designed by her and made up exclusively for the apartment. Then, when the apartment was finally completed, on the day she had planned to move in, her husband Marcelin died. She did not move in. Very occasionally she would host a dinner party there, but otherwise the apartment was kept almost as a shrine until the last years of her life, when her failing health obliged her to live there as it was more convenient.

Michel Castaing had been devoted to his mother, and knowing all that this place represented for her was torn apart at having to sell it. He told Marc that the apartment meant less to his own children than it did to us – strangers, who clearly loved it as much as he did, and wanted to preserve it. For two years he had been turning buyers away, even though the place was for sale; now he felt that the apartment had been waiting for us.

Marc told me later that Monsieur Castaing reminded him of his grandfather, and he felt great warmth towards him. Marc increased our offer. It was still one million francs less than the price Monsieur Castaing was expecting to achieve, but now he wanted us to have it and no one else. Marc called me in New York to tell me the news. I was extremely happy and excited. 'This is the place we were meant to have,' I said, and we agreed that as Angelo Manzolini had been responsible for bringing us to the place he would eventually restore it.

Now my only problem was telling Jim about this. Marc had faxed me an article that had recently appeared in the French press describing Madeleine Castaing's apartment and its historic and artistic importance, which is exactly the sort of thing that appeals to Jim. I showed Jim the article and he was intrigued. He asked a few of his friends about Madeleine Castaing, and his attitude began to change. I could now sense a hidden enthusiasm when we discussed the apartment. But I didn't tell him that I had actually bought the place. I was sure he would think I was being impulsive and hadn't considered the matter thoroughly enough.

However I didn't hesitate to call Jeanne. 'Bravo,' she said warmly. Few people, she added, have the ability to focus with such concentration on what they want to achieve and then make it happen. For all that, there was a sense of destiny about this whole adventure: there seemed to be a mystic quality in the connection between Jeanne, the apartment and the film.

According to French law three months must elapse between paying the deposit on a property and signing the final completion papers when the property becomes legally yours. As this was now the end of October, we could not expect to move into the new apartment before the end of January, which meant that we would either have to find another place to rent or move into a hotel. I phoned Marc to ask if there was any way we could move into Madeleine Castaing's apartment earlier. He was very doubtful, but he agreed to ask Michel Castaing, with whom he had established a close relationship.

Michel Castaing spoke with his lawyers about our request and they advised him that he would be crazy to allow us to occupy the apartment before completion of the sale. In addition, there was the matter of the antiques and, above all, the valuable Soutines. Michel Castaing called Marc in some agitation – on the one hand he knew it was totally irresponsible to allow us access to the place, but on the other he now felt complete confidence in us. Marc proposed we should pay for additional insurance on the art collection, but Michel Castaing pointed out that the premiums would obviously be prohibitive. Yes, he decided finally we could use the apartment and there would be no rental to pay, no extra insurance. He trusted us.

The furniture, the paintings, everything would remain in the apartment until the time came for it to be cleared. And, for the present, Mamadu and his wife Sahita would continue to act as housekeepers. We arranged for the china, crystal and other fragile articles to be taken away and stored because we didn't want to risk any accidental breakages. So while the other inhabitants of Paris were busy buying seasonal gifts, our Christmas shopping consisted of buying basic kitchenware and appliances.

On the night we moved in I cooked dinner for my associates, Humbert Balsan, Marc and Jim, who was now resigned to the fact that I had bought the apartment. We drank a toast to Madeleine Castaing resting in some wonderful part of heaven which she had probably redesigned in her own inimitable style. It was an incredible feeling to be living amongst her rare treasures, exactly as she had planned. There was only one drawback to this otherwise ideal arrangement – the notorious alarms.

Obviously there was a complex alarm system throughout the apartment, which also extended to cover the shop. The alarms operated automatically from eleven o'clock at night, after which we could not enter the building from the main entrance unless we were prepared to grapple with a series of intricate code-breaking manoeuvres. We had to use the servants' entrance, which had a simpler deactivating system. At first we frequently forgot about this arrangement and attempted to enter by the main entrance, only to jump out of our skins as the shrill sirens resonated all around us – the apartment, the shop, the whole street seemed to be wired to the alarms. Poor Mamadu had to get up to turn off the alarms and re-set the system. And the neighbours would throw open their windows, expecting to witness some daring heist, only to find two film-makers sneaking sheepishly into their house. In this way the valuable Soutines began to make our lives very difficult: instead of being a source of pleasure they had become a chronic pain.

Apart from that, we settled comfortably into our new home and on Christmas Day 1994 we had our first official dinner party. There were eighteen guests of different nationalities, so I decided to cook a multinational feast: turkey, Indian dishes, Christmas pudding and *bûche de Noël* sat side by side on the table with many, many bottles of champagne.

On New Year's Eve we were invited to a party given by the stage producer Laura Pels and her associate Gil Donaldson, who is an old friend of ours. Jeanne, Jim, Marc, my nephew Nayeem (who works as my assistant and has directed a film of his own) and some other friends marched like an army in the bitter cold to Laura's home on rue de l'Université.

As a surprise entertainment, Laura had arranged for a Tarot reader to come and tell us our future for the year ahead. The Tarot reader was put in the maid's room, which was small and unventilated. One by one the guests entered the room in great spirits, only to emerge a short while later with long miserable faces. The Tarot reader predicted doom for each of them, including Marc and the actress Marisa Berenson. By the time Jeanne went in, the atmosphere in the airless room had become so oppressive that she almost passed out. Then the Tarot reader suddenly became hysterical as she realized that Jeanne reminded her of her brother. Jeanne's future too, according to the cards, looked very bleak. Gloom descended on the party. What a way to begin the new year, I thought. It seemed that the only person who could look forward to a happy and prosperous year was our hostess, Laura Pels, for whom the cards predicted great things. In the event, however, we all enjoyed a very successful year in 1995. So much for Tarot cards.

At the end of January we took official possession of Madeleine Castaing's apartment. We went to the notary's office to sign the final papers and pay the balance of the money. It was a difficult moment for Michel Castaing, but he told us that although he had been reluctant to sell, he was happy that the apartment had come to us. He knew it would be in good hands.

THE SEARCH FOR A SCRIPT

The new year also brought the latest draft of Jean-Marie Besset's screenplay. It still didn't seem entirely right to me, but I sent it to Jeanne on 23 January (which is her birthday) for her comments. Jeanne had some concerns about the story and felt it didn't quite work. I agreed with her assessment. Besset was also having some difficulties creating the American characters, and I decided it might be useful to bring in an American writer. I sent the screenplay to George Trow who used to be a writer on the *New Yorker* magazine and is the author of a number of stage plays and books. George had also scripted our 1972 film *Savages*. He agreed to work on the screenplay.

The story that was finally devised for our film – now called *The Proprietor* – centred on Adrienne Mark, a celebrated French novelist who, at the height of her success in the 1960s, left Paris for New York where she spends the next thirty years. A growing disenchantment with that city makes her restless, and her work is becoming stale. The news that her mother's apartment in Paris, her own childhood home, is being auctioned provides the impulse for her return. She sells her home in New York and all her possessions, except for a valuable painting which she gives to her housekeeper, Milly, who is also her friend and confidante. Before she leaves the city she encounters a young media student, William O'Hara, who wants to make a video about her.

Adrienne is welcomed back to Paris by her ex-husband Elliott Spencer, her old admirer Raymond, and her close friend the film director Franz Legendre, who filmed her first novel in the 1960s, and who is now old and sick and cared for by his son Patrice. In order to pay for his father's medical costs, Patrice has agreed to let one of his father's most famous films be remade by a Hollywood studio headed by the brash movie executive Virginia Kelly. Franz Legendre's film of Adrienne's early novel had also been the subject of a Hollywood remake in the 1970s, which turned out to be a travesty of the original film. Patrice hopes that Adrienne can exert some influence over Virginia Kelly to avoid the present film suffering the same fate as his father's earlier film.

Adrienne, however, must also confront the ghosts of her past. Her mother, Judith Mark, a Jewish *couturière*, had been betrayed by her lover during the war and taken from her apartment by the Nazis. Adrienne never saw her mother again, and her life has been haunted by the thought that she might have been able to save her.

After Adrienne's failure to buy her mother's apartment at the auction, Milly, unknown to her, sells the portrait she had been given and provides the additional money which secures the apartment for Adrienne. Meanwhile, the devotion and respect shown to Franz Legendre by Patrice and Adrienne gives Virginia Kelly a different perspective on the film she intends to make. And William O'Hara arrives in Paris to pursue his documentary.

As Adrienne reconciles the past to her new life in Paris, she discovers that she still loves her ex-husband Elliott and, above all, that she can write again. With the ghosts of the past laid to rest, the story closes at the Cannes Film Festival where Adrienne is honoured with a special award.

And I didn't even want to think about how much it would cost to stage the final scene with the thousands of extras it would involve.

I had hoped that George Trow could iron out the problems which existed in the present script, so I eagerly read through his draft when it arrived. Alas, it was still not quite right. He had improved the first half – the part set in New York. And he had developed the relationship between Adrienne and Milly, which I considered a very important element in the story. But he had not integrated the changes he had made to the first part into the second part, and therefore the piece lacked a consistency of tone, and now seemed unbalanced and somehow incomplete.

George is one hell of a writer and I have the greatest admiration for his work. However, his style sometimes tends to the elliptical or obscure – an approach that can work brilliantly with less naturalistic narratives, but I felt our story needed to be told more directly and simply. Until we had a strong script that we could send out to potential investors there was no possibility of raising any money for the film. Getting a decent script had therefore become a matter of urgency. George came to Paris to work on the script with me, and each day he would come to the apartment from his hotel around the corner.

As a film-maker my life has been dominated by scripts, but I have never written one myself because I have never needed to. In Ruth Prawer Jhabvala I have the best script-writer. Screenplays are an area of film-making I leave entirely to Ruth and Jim, and I don't interfere. I became involved in the script for *In Custody*, but that was in many ways easier because we were working from a novel. This time, however, I was becoming very frustrated with the process because, although I can write dialogue I can't, for example, structure it to an eight-page scene. I knew when it wasn't working, when it didn't sound right, when it seemed artificial or lacked conviction – but I had to depend on a writer to give me what I felt it needed, to get the right tone.

Ruth was still busy with her own work, but she generously sacrificed some time to give us a number of very helpful notes which really steered us in the right direction, and she was always prepared to advise us whenever we needed her assistance. Jim, too, made valuable contributions to the script. Their experience in this field has given them an aptitude – a genius almost – for telling a story through its characters.

In the middle of all this the remover came to clear out the Madeleine Castaing's furniture and belongings. I had arranged with Michael Castaing to buy a few of the pieces I liked – and some other pieces were also being left behind to be returned after the film. Our original intention had been to shoot the film in the apartment as it existed but in the end this was not practical. Although the rooms were large, they were filled with furniture and objects, and there was no way the remaining space could accommodate cast, crew and bulky film equipment. We could, however, rely on the existing architectural details to capture the style and ambience of Madeleine Castaing's apartment for our story.

RAISING THE MONEY, ASSEMBLING THE CAST

By March 1995 we finally had an acceptable script which we could send to Eurimages, the European body that partially funds films. The script still needed some fine tuning, but we felt confident that it was now strong enough to send out for finance. Humbert Balsan prepared a budget, and I went into battle with Jeanne's agent. Jeanne's fee is, understandably, in the upper range. She is, after all, a great actress and a valuable asset to any film. Our budget, however, was only $5.8 million so we couldn't afford any huge salaries. Fortunately, we came to a satisfactory agreement, though it was all academic – we hadn't yet raised a sou to make the film. The idea of approaching Eurimages had come from Premila Hoon of Guiness Mahon, the Merchant Bank which underwrites our loans. Premila had also recommended we should use Mo Yusuf, a lawyer who is very experienced in putting such deals together.

In order to qualify for Eurimages money three European countries have to be involved in the film, and we had only two – Merchant Ivory from England and Ognon Films, Humbert's company, from France. We approached certain film companies in Italy and Germany, but as the film had no national interest for them they saw no point in getting involved. I found out that Turkey qualified for Eurimages funding, so I telephoned Osman Eralp, a Turkish friend who works for Polygram Records and who had been wanting to get into the movie business. 'Osman,' I said, 'your time has come to get into the motion picture business – you will be the executive producer on our new film.' Osman managed to form a Turkish company virtually overnight, and with the three-nation partnership in place we prepared our application for Eurimages: thirty-five copies of the script, thirty-five copies of the budget, thirty-five synopses of the film, thirty-five copies of Jeanne's contract, statements from the director, biographies, the commitment of Peter Elson at Largo, our American sales agent – a mountain of paper had been assembled.

We had cut the timing of our application so fine that the only way of getting all this to Eurimages before the deadline closed was for Marc Tissot to drive like a demon all the way to Strasbourg. He screeched to a halt in front of the Eurimages office at 5.15 p.m. The deadline was 5.30 p.m. – we had just made it. The application was accepted, but we wouldn't know for some weeks whether they would grant us any money towards the film.

The Eurimages money would be very useful, but the sum we could expect would still be a long way short of the $5.8 million we needed to raise, so we began to send proposals to various distributors and television channels who might provide some investment. The obvious place to start was with Canal Plus, which is the French equivalent of Britain's Channel 4 in that part of its remit is to finance and showcase independent films. The reader gave the script a poor report, but Nathalie Bloch-Lainé, the director of buying, intended to read the script herself before making a final decision. Executives never usually read the scripts that are sent to them, basing their decisions instead on a reader's report. If this is prepared by someone ill-equipped for the job, a worthwhile project can die before it's given a chance.

Aware of this, we didn't, of course, just sit back. Humbert and I went to see Nathalie to make sure that she *would* read the script. We bombarded her with the film's qualities – its humour, its emotional depth, the interconnecting plots – and Humbert, who oozes Gallic charm and finesse to finagle his way to his objective, didn't let up until Nathalie agreed to read the script. I have always been considered a master at charming people into submission, but on the evidence of this performance Humbert's capabilities could exceed even my best efforts – though, of course, he's learnt almost everything he knows from me.

We needed to start shooting *The Proprietor* in May because it had to be completed by August if we were to avoid clashing with the shooting of *Surviving Picasso*, which was scheduled to start in September. Already Jim was expressing anxiety about my involvement with *The Proprietor* and he was uncomfortable about the close timing of the two projects. I knew that I could direct *The Proprietor* and produce *Surviving Picasso*, but that didn't reassure Jim.

It wasn't going to be easy to do both, but it was possible. And then Jeanne called to tell me that she had been appointed President of the Jury for the 1995 Cannes Film Festival. That would certainly interfere with our shooting schedule for *The Proprietor* and make the space between the two films even tighter. But Cannes is an important event, so I told Jeanne we could postpone our shooting until after she had completed her commitment to the festival.

Jeanne had had some professional disappointments in recent years: a couple of films she was to have directed had fallen apart, and in one case she had lost some money, and other projects she was involved with failed to materialize at the last moment, as is often the case with films. I knew she was as eager to begin work on *The Proprietor* as I was. A few weeks delay may not seem much, but it would bring us too close to the Picasso film.

Instead of being alarmed by the news of her Cannes appointment, however, I was tremendously excited. The expensive Cannes sequence in *The Proprietor* could, I realized, now cost me very little. Merchant Ivory would be participating in the festival as *Jefferson in Paris* was being shown in competition. And now Jeanne would be there as President of the Jury. Instead of having to pay thousands of extras to represent the crowds and photographers, I could shoot the real event with Jeanne – or Adrienne – quite legitimately in their midst.

During the process of writing the script I had mentally cast some of the parts, and now that shooting at Cannes was imminent I approached individual actors – even though we hadn't yet raised any money to make the film.

Christopher Cazenove, the versatile British stage and screen actor whose credits range from *Hamlet* on stage to *Dynasty* on television, agreed to play the part of Elliott Spencer, Adrienne's ex-husband. Christopher had starred in our film *Heat and Dust* in 1982 and I was looking forward to working with him again. Sean Young, another Merchant Ivory alumna, was to play the movie executive Virginia Kelly. Sean made her screen début in our 1980 film *Jane Austen in Manhattan* and went on to work with a number of interesting directors including Oliver Stone in *Wall Street*, David Lynch in *Dune* and Ridley Scott in *Blade Runner*.

For the part of Franz Legendre we cast Jean-Pierre Aumont, one of France's most distinguished actors, who had just worked with us on *Jefferson*. In his long career he has triumphed on both the French and American stage, and on screen in such popular films as Truffaut's *Day for Night* and Lelouch's *Cat and Mouse*. Marc Tissot was to play his son Patrice. Along with Jeanne as Adrienne, Marc was the first to be cast in the film.

Pierre Vaneck, well known in France for his numerous television appearances as well as his stage and screen work, came to see me for the part of Raymond, Adrienne's old admirer. Vaneck was on the board of La Centre National du Cinéma, another source to which we had applied for finance for the film. Although Vaneck had liked the script very much and had tried to persuade the Centre to put up some of the money, they turned us down on the grounds that *The Proprietor* was not a French-language film. In fact it is a bilingual film and carries French nationality, so I thought their attitude was rather provincial, but we weren't discouraged.

We had to work around Vaneck's existing schedule because he had already been cast in Oliver Parker's film of *Othello*, which was shooting in Rome at the same time as *The Proprietor*. A number of our friends were involved in that film, so during shooting Vaneck became a kind of messenger, passing news and gossip between the two sets as he travelled to and fro between Paris and Rome.

Things were progressing smoothly when Jeanne called to tell me that since I became involved in her life her luck had changed – more offers of films and plays had started coming her way, and there was one film she wanted to do whose dates clashed with ours. Filming was due to begin in New York and Germany, and Jeanne wanted to know if it would be possible for her to do both that film and *The Proprietor*. I told Jeanne to accept the other film as we could try and work our schedule around her. In fact I had absolutely no idea whether, or even how, that would be possible, but I didn't want Jeanne to turn down a part she wanted to do. On paper, at least, there was still a question mark over *The Proprietor* as we hadn't yet raised any money. But I never had any doubts that we would make this film. Somehow it would happen.

Things were still in that uncertain state when Jim and I flew to New York for the opening of *Jefferson in Paris*. The film wasn't the success we had hoped for in the United States, and in the light of the poor critical response there the Cannes Film Festival committee were considering removing the film from the competition. The committee had seen the completed film before its release and had thought it worthy of a place in the festival, so this was a disappointment for us. Irrespective of their final decision, however, we were going ahead with our preparations for Cannes. Months earlier we had arranged to rent a beautiful villa in Antibes for the duration of the festival and also to use as a location for *The Proprietor*, so we would still shoot our Cannes sequence there.

The committee finally decided that *Jefferson* would remain in the competition, and hard on the heels of that news we also heard that Eurimages had granted us $600,000 towards *The Proprietor*, having given me the status of honorary European citizen.

We started to hire technicians, the costume and production designers, hair and make-up people, and the cinematographer – the director's right-hand man. The cinematographer, also known as the director of photography or more commonly the cameraman, is responsible for realizing the director's vision in practical terms – which often isn't easy. In a film the cinematography works like a visual counterpoint to the music. It must create mood, suggest nuance, and underline key moments in subtle ways. To achieve this the cinematographer dictates the lighting, and works with the director to find the best angles, the best approach to maximize the impact of each scene. If it's done well the technique goes unnoticed – but not the effect.

I very much wanted Larry Pizer for this film. One of the most experienced and talented cinematographers in the business, with a formidable list of credits, he had shot *The Europeans* for us and had also worked on *Jefferson in Paris* and *Mr and Mrs Bridge* as an additional cameraman. He was the cinematographer on my first film as director *In Custody*, and I will always be grateful for his contribution. His guidance steered me away from major technical errors, and he always responded positively to my ideas – no matter how crazy they seemed. Larry is a truly wonderful collaborator with a steady temper, a great sense of humour, and a down-to-earth, flexible approach to his work. I am certain that working with a less understanding cinematographer would, sooner or later, result in a fist fight between us.

I also began to think about the music for the film and called our long-time collaborator and friend Richard Robbins, the American composer who has been scoring our films for twenty years. Dick is another truly gifted individual. Although his background is in classical music, he has an extraordinary flair for film work. His scores never fail to find the musical equivalent of the script's narrative tone, and his remarkable talents have been recognized with many awards including two Oscar nominations for his work on *Howards End* and *The Remains of the Day*. When Dick had been in Paris earlier in the year working on the music for *Jefferson*, I had asked him to listen to a recording of the concert given by the soprano Barbara Hendricks in aid of Sarajevo. I thought her voice was one of the most beautiful and expressive I had ever heard, and suggested to Dick we should consider using Hendricks on the soundtrack of *The Proprietor*. Dick liked the idea, so I sent a fax to Hendricks in Geneva, where she lives, requesting a meeting with her.

On the same day a fax arrived from Barbara Hendricks – who had not yet received my fax – requesting a meeting with me on an entirely different matter. She wanted to discuss a project she was planning on the great black contralto Marian Anderson, who had been prevented on racist grounds from singing at the Met in New York until 1955 when, at the age of fifty-three, she finally made her début there as Ulrica in *Un Ballo in Maschera*. (I had actually heard Anderson sing in Bombay some forty-five years ago.)

When Barbara Hendricks came to Paris I invited her to the apartment, then took her to dinner at the Restaurant Voltaire on the Quai Voltaire, where we were joined by Marc, whose home is also in Geneva. Over dinner, however, our conversation was dominated not by Geneva, nor by the music for *The Proprietor* or even by Marian Anderson, but by the extraordinarily coincidental timing of our faxes.

CANNES CONNECTIONS

We arrived in Cannes on 15 May, the day before the 1995 festival opened. And for the next two weeks I had to perform a dual role – producer of *Jefferson in Paris*, which I had to promote, and director of *The Proprietor*, which I had to begin shooting. As well as the stars of *Jefferson*, which included Nick Nolte and Greta Scacchi, we had also brought with us the actors involved in the Cannes sequences of *The Proprietor* – Jean-Pierre Aumont, Christopher Cazenove, Marc Tissot and Sean Young.

I also met for the first time the actor who was to play the part of William O'Hara, the young media student who follows Adrienne Mark from New York to Paris. Normally a director meets his leading actors before they are cast, but I had not seen anyone who seemed right for that part during casting sessions in New York. Then, with time running out, I asked Donald Rosenfeld, my associate in New York and one of the producers of *The Proprietor*, to send me photographs of suitable actors, from which I picked Josh Hamilton. It's not the conventional way of casting an important character for a film, and the first time I actually set eyes on Josh was in Cannes, only one day before the shooting. Luckily he was perfect.

Jeanne was at Cannes in her official capacity and not as part of the Merchant Ivory team. Nevertheless, the fact that the President of the Jury was to sit in judgement on a film made by the people she was about to work with provoked murmurs of conflict of interest. This was absolute nonsense – Jeanne is a person of the highest integrity. And as for us, we've been around long enough to know that films stand or fall on their own merit. For the record, *Jefferson* won no prizes at Cannes.

Peter Elson, our American sales agent, also arrived, bringing glossy brochures and other promotional literature advertising *The Proprietor*. The chief purpose of the Cannes Festival, despite its public image, is as a film market, and while the stars pose for the paparazzi on the Croisette, distributors, financiers and producers spend their days in hotel suites, offices and screening rooms, buying, selling and making deals. This trading also continues into the night at numerous parties and receptions. It was imperative to raise some interest in *The Proprietor* during Cannes: on the eve of shooting we had only the Eurimages money and a commitment from Peter's company, Largo.

My first priority in Cannes was to see Gilles Jacob, the director of the festival, to get permission to shoot the opening of the festival. Humbert had already approached the press liaison, but they would only allow us to erect one camera, and we needed to use three. We also needed to infiltrate our own actors into the official arrival of the jury on the opening night.

Getting to see Gilles Jacob is never easy. This year it was even more difficult because the government had fallen just a few days earlier and everything was in chaos. So I took an armful of Merchant Ivory books and barged into his offices, using the books to bribe anyone who looked as though they might be able to get me into Monsieur Jacob's inner sanctum. Once there, however, I found Monsieur Jacob responding to each of my requests with a terse 'impossible'. Well, we would see.

The following morning I took my cast (with the exception of Jeanne) and the three cameras to the Palais du Festival for a rehearsal. We positioned the actors, sited the cameras, and everything looked as if it would work. However, although I had attended the festival many times, now, in my capacity as a director, I somehow managed to overlook the reality of how the situation would be that night – the thousands of people solidly blocking the area around the Palais, the banks of photographers with whom we would have to battle for space, and the fact that there would be only one chance to capture this scene on the film.

The official schedule for the opening night was that the jury and its President would meet at the Majestic Hotel from where they would be driven to the Palais in the festival cars, pennants flying. Traditionally, the Minister of Culture and other ministers follow. I had persuaded the person responsible for the festival transport to give us two official cars, and I intended to intercept the ministerial cars and follow the jury in the processional drive to the Palais. When the jury, led by Jeanne Moreau, ascended the broad red-carpeted stairway to the entrance of the Palais, our cast would be directly behind. Adrienne Mark would arrive at this ceremony accompanied by her friends, not officials or ministers. By another lucky chance the Nobel Prize winning novelist Nadine Gordimer was also on the jury, and it would be highly appropriate for Adrienne to be in the company of another important writer. Of course none of the jury, apart from Jeanne, had any idea of what we were up to.

I had taken my position next to Larry Pizer on the steps outside the Palais in anticipation of the arrival of the procession. Jeanne, who had not been told where the cameras were, emerged from the first car and waited while the rest of the jury assembled around her, closely followed by our cast. As they all began to walk towards the steps, Jeanne, for the briefest moment, imperceptibly slipped out of her role as President of the Jury and into the character of Adrienne Mark: she half-turned and gently kissed Christopher Cazenove's face. It was a perfect gesture towards Elliott for the film, yet it appeared to be just a simple acknowledgement of one actor by another.

And then all hell broke loose. The crowds started calling Jean-Pierre Aumont's name as he followed the procession, and Jean-Pierre completely forgot we were shooting this scene for the film. Enthusiastically responding to the crowd, he bounded energetically up the stairs to greet the festival committee at the top. In the film Jean-Pierre as Franz Legendre is an old man recovering from a stroke, but here he was moving like an Olympic athlete. I ran up the stairs to stop him, but it was too late. Jean-Pierre had disappeared into the Palais with Jeanne and the jury, and there was no time to look for him in that mass of people. By now, the photographers were shouting for Sean Young, who was ascending the stairs with Marc, ahead of the other celebrities and officials including the recently appointed Minister of Culture, Monsieur Douste-Blazy, escorting Barbara Hendricks. I ran down the stairs yelling at everyone to stop and they were so amazed at the sight of this crazy Indian that they obeyed.

We did another take with my depleted cast and some very perplexed officials, and trusted that we could cut the footage together in the editing room. One way or another, I knew we had a very good 'production value' shot in the can – a 'million-dollar' shot, in fact. So, despite the confusion, there were lots of smiles as I assumed my official place at the end of the procession for the opening ceremony.

Buyers now started to appear at Peter Elson's office to take up rights on *The Proprietor*. There was a lot of interest from David Aukin of Channel 4, and this was both encouraging and gratifying as our association with the channel goes back to its inception. David has always been a supporter and champion of quality films, and a man like that is very important for independent producers. Peter Smith of Polygram showed similar interest, and Nathalie Bloch-Lainé, who had now read the script and saw its potential, committed on behalf of Canal Plus. The money was slowly coming together, and every day I would go to Peter's office to see what progress was being made. If buyers were haggling over the price I would tell them about the million-dollar shot which they were getting for free.

After the adventures of the opening night we settled into the normal Cannes routine of watching movies and attending parties. Cannes is devoted to film for only two weeks of the year; the rest of the time it is a playground for the wealthy, though during the festival fortnight the two sides tend to mingle. One evening Greta Scacchi, Marc and I were invited to a dinner party aboard the yacht of a Saudi Arabian prince, where I met yet another Saudi prince who in turn invited the three of us to *his* yacht. So, a few days later, the prince's motor launch collected us from the marina at Cannes and transported us to yet another yacht.

More of a floating palace than a yacht, it was vast, elegantly contemporary in style, and surprisingly understated – the kind of understatement that costs millions to achieve. The prince was charming, and we got along very well. He showed us a fascinating video he had shot in Jeddah of himself hand-feeding sharks, much of it shot underwater and really quite daring. We were all very impressed, and while we were discussing films I mentioned *The Proprietor* and invited him to come to the set when we started shooting. Unfortunately, he was planning to leave Cannes before that time, but we exchanged addresses and he asked me to send him a proposal about *The Proprietor*.

In Cannes I also managed to cast the part of Adrienne's mother, Judith. I had seen a number of actresses for this important role, but my indecision indicated that none of them was exactly right. At the party we gave on the night *Jefferson* was shown Charlotte de Turckheim, who had played Marie Antoinette in that film, was telling us about her press interviews at Cannes. While she was talking to me, I realized that she could be a brilliant choice for Adrienne's mother. 'Charlotte,' I asked, 'would you like to be in another Merchant Ivory film? But this time it will be directed by me and you will play Jeanne Moreau's mother.' Charlotte looked surprised (she is some years younger than Jeanne), but when I explained that Adrienne's mother is seen only in flashback with Adrienne as a child, she agreed.

During the Cannes festival you frequently receive invitations from (and issue them to) people you don't know. So it didn't seem odd when, out of the blue, the fashion designer Nino Cerruti asked me to lunch. I have, from time to time, bought Cerruti clothes for my own wardrobe, and I was looking forward to this meeting. I found Nino tremendously *simpatico*, as the Italians say, and when I suggested he might design some special clothes for Jeanne to wear in *The Proprietor* he responded with great enthusiasm. Our costume designer for the film was Anne de Laugardière, in whom I had tremendous confidence, but Jeanne, who was unfamiliar with Anne's work, seemed a little nervous about some of the early sketches. I thought that Jeanne would feel more comfortable with Cerruti's elegant, classic styles.

My interest in the costumes, wigs and make-up for films extends only to their cost – which I always regard as too high, and sometimes I get annoyed with Jim for spending so much time and money on those aspects. This attitude was, I felt, amply justified by my experience when I directed *In Custody* – a few conferences with the costume designer about styles and colours was all that was needed. I didn't take into account that saris and kurtas are a lot easier to deal with than the intricacies of period costume or, as in the present case, that the tastes of the actors influence how they choose to look in contemporary films.

As a producer I have always done my best to make the actors comfortable and happy; as a director, however, you have to do even more. Now I was learning how important every aspect, every insignificant detail of costume, hair and make-up was to an actor preparing to assume the shape of a character. And because these elements had already caused some friction between Jeanne and the production, I made it my business to attend costume fittings and concern myself with the details of even the tiniest accessory.

The problems had begun back in Paris. Jeanne wanted to appoint her own make-up designer to work on the film, but when Humbert tried to negotiate the deal the make-up designer complained to Jeanne that she had been insulted by our low offer, and Jeanne was very upset. Humbert couldn't offer more because he didn't want to discriminate against the rest of the crew who were on basic rates. I went to see Jeanne about all this, and I was surprised by her change of tone towards me. I had been warned that Jeanne can be temperamental when her authority is challenged, and now there was irritation in her voice because she thought I was taking this matter too lightly. She was wrong. I was only too aware, inconceivable though it might seem, that this whole production could collapse because of a dispute over who should apply the pancake. God knows, films have come to grief on less than that.

When you are dealing with a strong-minded person you have to be especially delicate and diplomatic, otherwise the situation can get explosive. Fortunately, the matter was resolved during the Cannes festival, where Jeanne was the subject of a Canal Plus television documentary. Her make-up for this, and other events at Cannes, was being done by Nicola Degennes, a talented French make-up artist. I met Nicola Degennes and thought he would fit in well with the team we had assembled, which eventually included Fernando, a brilliant and unflappable hair stylist whom Jeanne had recommended.

One of the dresses being designed by Anne de Laugardière in Paris for Jeanne was ready for the first fitting, but as Jeanne could not leave Cannes during the festival, the dress and its maker had to come to us. I had already decided on a specific look for Adrienne: as a writer her focus would be internal rather than external, so she would dress simply and elegantly. Jeanne is very particular about her clothes, and at first she did not trust that Anne would create the look she wanted. I made a point of attending this fitting because I felt the situation might demand a referee.

The dress was a glorious peach-coloured affair that Adrienne was to wear in Cannes, where she should look like a Greek goddess, a mythical creature. This fluid and elegant creation was just perfect, and Jeanne was happy in it. But neither Jeanne nor I liked the brooch which accompanied it.

On the last Saturday of the festival Anne and I went to the shops to try and find a more suitable brooch for the dress, and as we walked along the Croisette we suddenly saw it in the window of Van Cleef and Arpels; an unusual art-deco style brooch of pale pink coral shaped like a bow, rimmed with diamonds, and encrusted in amethysts set into blue and green enamel. 'Well, we must have it,' I said. Anne responded that it would probably cost more than the entire budget of the film. 'But Anne,' I replied, 'I don't intend to *buy* it.'

Like most expensive jewellers the shop was locked and we had to ring and wait while they looked us over. We were allowed inside, and I asked if it might be possible to borrow the brooch in the window to use in a film. I was told that such a transaction could only be authorized by their head office in Paris, and we were asked to return the following day.

The Paris office gave its permission on condition that the brooch be returned immediately after the shoot. As a precaution they also asked for my credit card number. I wasn't carrying any credit cards and the shop was about to close for lunch, so we arranged that I would return later that afternoon when they reopened. Any time before seven, I was told, when they shut.

We had to shoot some additional footage of crowd scenes that night – the last night of the festival – so that evening we returned to the Palais and set up our cameras amidst another huge crowd. When you are filming you are completely unaware of time, and I practically jumped out of my skin when I realized it was just a few minutes before seven and Van Cleef and Arpels was about to close; so I leapt down the Palais stairs, yelling to Larry to take over, then ran all the way along the Croisette, arriving breathless at Van Cleef and Arpels just as they were bringing down the heavy metal security grille. I waved my credit card at the window, the grille went up, they let me in, took an imprint of my card, and I grabbed the brooch and ran back to the Palais to finish the remaining shots.

The next day we were to shoot one of our major sequences. This involved a total of fourteen different set-ups to be shot in a single day, so the schedule was extremely tight. The set was the Villa Nerellic in Antibes which we had rented from the politician Jacqueline Patenotre and where we had been staying for the duration of the festival. By the time we were due to start work, however, the place was nowhere near ready for shooting – people were still having breakfast, the crew were trying to clear space in the bedrooms for the wardrobe and make-up departments, and there was an atmosphere of chaos everywhere. In the middle of all this activity Jeanne arrived and came face to face for the first time with the crazy world of Merchant Ivory film-making, which she seemed to view with some disapproval.

Much as I had longed for the chance of making a film with Jeanne, and despite her support and enthusiasm for this project, I knew that working with her would not be easy. As well as being a uniquely gifted actress and a very experienced one, Jeanne brings an awesome depth and breadth to the characters she plays, colouring them with complexities unimagined on the printed page. And I had to accept that you don't achieve those results without strong, firm ideas about character and story. But film-making is a collaborative effort and everyone involved must exercise a degree of flexibility. I hoped that the understanding that had grown between us would keep things smooth.

And so we began. What had started, as usual, in chaos, ended late that night with all the shots. Much of the credit for that must go to Larry. His experience and no-nonsense approach to his work ensured that we covered all fourteen set-ups with the minimum delay. And we celebrated with a wonderful dinner for everyone at Quattro Fontane, an Italian restaurant in Antibes.

Before leaving Cannes I went back to Van Cleef and Arpels – not to return the brooch, however, but to try and persuade them to let us keep it for the duration of the shooting. That piece of jewellery, so right in terms of period and individual style, had inspired another idea – that the brooch had belonged to Adrienne's mother, becoming the only, treasured memento Adrienne has of her. Van Cleef and Arpels agreed to this extended loan, and we were allowed to take the brooch from Cannes to Paris to New York, and back again.

After Cannes there was to be a five-week hiatus in the shooting while Jeanne completed her other film, and so the following day everyone dispersed to their various destinations, and I set off on the long drive back to Paris. I was disappointed that *Jefferson* hadn't done well at Cannes, but that disappointment was balanced by the progress we had made on *The Proprietor* – the film that had come from nowhere and had taken on a life of its own. Admittedly, the script was still incomplete and in need of a lot more work, parts were still to be cast and locations found, the money was still not in place – and yet we had already completed one entire part of the film.

PARIS, VERSAILLES AND THE VAL D'OISE, SUMMER 1995

The route from my apartment on rue Bonaparte to our office in rue Montmartre covers some of the finest Parisian landmarks – the Ecole des Beaux Arts, the Académie Française, the Pont Neuf and the Louvre. At any time of the year, even in midwinter, but especially in spring and summer when the trees are in bloom and the sunlight sparkles on the Seine, these sights have a magic of their own and the stroll to work always puts me in good spirits. I was in just such a mood one morning when I arrived in the office to be told there was a Zurich banker on the telephone wanting to speak with me. Every film producer dreams of calls from Swiss bankers but that rarely happens, so I was very intrigued.

The Zurich banker was calling on the instructions of the Saudi prince to whom I had sent the proposal. He asked for more information about the film, so we sent him everything he asked for, not entirely sure that we'd ever hear from him again. A few days later, however, he called back to tell us that he had been authorized by his client to put up a portion of the budget for the film and appoint lawyers to undertake the negotiations. We contacted Mo Yusuf, the lawyer who had negotiated our deal with Eurimages, to act on our behalf and within a matter of days the deal was settled.

There was a lot to be done during the five weeks before we commenced shooting in Paris. I called on Nino Cerruti to finalize the details of the clothes he was preparing for Jeanne, and the arrangements being made for the other actors. While Jeanne would enjoy the luxury of dresses designed exclusively for her by Nino, the rest of the cast were also rather spoilt in that they would be allowed to choose their outfits from the *pret-à-porter* lines in the Cerruti collection. All Nino wanted to know was how much time he was being given to complete the work on Jeanne's outfits. 'Four, five weeks?' I suggested optimistically. Nino's assistants protested that it would be nowhere near enough time, but Nino ignored them. He was certain they would be ready and that we would be happy with them. This down-to-earth, efficient attitude, rare amongst the often precious personalities in the fashion world, is one I greatly admire.

In order to complete the work on time Nino established an atelier in Paris, rather than having the designs made up at his own atelier in Italy as is his usual practice. Thus he avoided the inevitable delays involved in transporting everything back and forth between fittings. As well as being a leading *couturier*, Nino had dressed the stars for a large number of major films including Sharon Stone in *Basic Instinct*, Robert Redford in *Indecent Proposal*, Tom Hanks in *Philadelphia* and Richard Gere in *Pretty Woman*. So he is aware of the demands and difficulties of the *métier* – not least the constant race against the clock. Anne de Laugardière had nothing but the highest praise for Nino and his colleagues, and told me she had never worked with such an efficient and helpful team.

I also began to look at various Paris locations. Friends are the best source of information about potential locations, and a number of friends had made suggestions about useful properties. We checked them all, but it didn't always work out as planned. When we went to look at a possible location for Elliott Spencer's apartment we found, instead, the location for Franz Legendre's home – *and* a completely new scene for the film. Sometimes locations inspire new ideas for the story or the characters, and if you are given an opportunity to maximize the use of a location by building up a scene in this way, you take it. Locations have a life of their own and enhance a film more than you can imagine – it has happened to us many times.

In this instance the inspirational location was the home of the Mexican painter Marie-Carmen Hernandez, who is known as Metha, and has a unique seventeenth-century apartment overlooking the gardens of the Place des Vosges. As soon as I saw it I knew it was exactly what we needed – not for Elliott, however, but for Franz and Patrice. Franz is meant to be a legendary figure, a film director of the stature of Jean Renoir. He would live in a place with an unusual quality, among the kind of books and paintings that would give his character substance.

I invited Metha to dinner one evening to negotiate. The price she was asking was very high and she was also concerned about the disruption – especially as she would be away at the time of shooting and there would be no one to keep an eye on us while we were there. Negotiations continued at a cocktail party that was given for me, and a friendship began to develop between us. By the time she invited me to lunch at her studio near the Odéon she had come to understand how much her home meant to us, and a reasonable deal was made.

Another vital location was the office suite for Virginia Kelly, the American movie executive. I had seen the penthouse boardroom at the top of the ultramodern Sony building on Avenue Wagram and it struck me as very appropriate – a vast space, plated glass on three sides opening on to broad terraces with olive trees and lavender growing in tubs, and a sweeping panorama of the city; it had just the right atmosphere of power and money that characterizes top movie executives.

Maxim's was a very specific location essential to the film. The crucial scene where Adrienne's mother, a Jew, signs over her apartment to her lover, a Gentile, in order to avoid having it confiscated by the Nazis during the occupation, has to take place at Maxim's. This is also the scene where the young Adrienne confronts anti-Semitism for the first time. Our difficulty here was that Pierre Cardin, who owns this historic restaurant, was asking for the kind of money that was completely out of our league. People always associate films with money; they read about huge budgets, the astronomical fees some actors can command, and the enormous profits some producers are fortunate to make. In reality, most independent films are made on modest budgets, and we had already pared down the costs of *The Proprietor* to the minimum. But in this case Maxim's was so representative of that period, of the place its clientele occupied in pre-war society, that there was no question of using an alternative. So Pierre Cardin got the price he wanted without making any concessions, leaving us to try and make savings elsewhere.

For Elliott Spencer's apartment I had already set my heart on the house of some friends of ours because it had a garden, and I felt that Elliott, as an Englishman, would naturally have a garden. Unfortunately, some work was due to be done to the house at the time of filming, so it wouldn't be possible. Our friend Véronique de Goldschmidt, who was very useful in tracking down locations for us (and even acted as an extra in one of the scenes), found a good substitute in rue Bayard near the Rond Point des Champs Elysées. Except that it didn't have a garden . . . Well, we would just have to find a garden elsewhere.

Another key location that was causing us some headaches was the one we needed for the film-within-the-film sequence where Adrienne watches a clip from the American remake of her filmed novel, *Call Me French*. Dating from the 1970s, this remake would have a particular Hollywood look. We had seen a number of apartments and hotels for this location but they all lacked the kind of atmosphere I was hoping to find. I gave Donald Rosenfeld, who had come to Paris from New York, the responsibility of scouting this particularly troublesome location. Together with Pamela Ballweg, who worked for Nino Cerruti and therefore had lots of contacts in the fashion industry, Donald went on a tour of all sorts of likely places. Finally, Pamela suggested using one of the boats or barges moored along the bank of the Seine near Pont Alexandre II. We went to see the boats and one of them seemed right – it even had a large fish tank in the *salon* which was a rather witty touch.

As well as this film clip, we also had to show another clip of Franz Legendre's original film of Adrienne's novel, made in the early 1960s. Everyone, including Jeanne and Jim, cautioned me to beware of these scenes. Impersonating Hollywood and, more especially, the French New Wave would be fraught with dangers: unless done with a great deal of thought, these scenes could end up as parodies rather than as evocations of the real thing. But I felt confident I could handle this material. I recalled the New Wave films I had seen when I first went to New York in 1958 as a student. The effects of seeing the work of Malle, Truffaut, Godard and Chabrol on someone whose experience of cinema had been limited to exaggeratedly overacted Hindi films and the fantasy world of imported Hollywood musicals can only be imagined.

With the New Wave films new vistas had opened up for me. I watched them over and over again, and was profoundly affected by them.

Four days before shooting started the cast assembled in the rue Bayard apartment for the first read-through of the script. I presented each member of the cast with a silver pen from Tiffany's for good luck: it is a Merchant Ivory tradition to start each film with a memento of the occasion.

As well as Ruth's and Jim's exemplary suggestions and comments on the script, Jim's assistant Andy Litvack provided some additional dialogue and scenes, and all these contributions were incorporated into the screenplay through its various drafts. But it isn't until you begin to work on the piece at a read-through that you get a real sense of which scenes will work and which won't. There were still problems with the script, and these sessions gave us an indication of what still needed to be done. Later, Jeanne told me how much she appreciated this 'democratic' process. The readings, the free exchange of ideas between cast and director, helped everyone to see things with greater clarity.

We would be working only five-day weeks, but those days would consist of between twelve and fourteen hours – sometimes more. Actors are always worried about the schedule, particularly when they are at the centre of the film, and even before we began Jeanne was apprehensive about the gruelling pace – anxious that the long hours would allow her no chance to prepare her work for the following day, or even to sleep. I told her that whenever she felt tired I would allow her to rest. I was lying – or rather, I would have liked to believe that I would have done that for Jeanne but we simply didn't have the time or money to sustain any delays. During shooting, however, Jeanne showed no signs of fatigue which, as she told me, was just as well because she knew that I would never have interrupted the work to allow her to rest.

Shooting began on 9 July 1995. In a street near the Académie des Beaux Arts we had assembled two hundred extras who were to stage a political demonstration against right-wing extremism. So, on the first day, I had to cope with a rioting, shouting, banner-waving mob, and a car with Adrienne, Elliott, Patrice and Virginia driving through this crowd.

I wanted to see the car pass through the rioters from a higher angle, so we went up to ask the people who lived in an apartment overlooking the street if they would allow us to shoot the scene from their balcony. We were surprised when they angrily turned us down, accusing us of staging a demonstration against the Right. I had never imagined that on the Left Bank people would support right-wing extremism, or be so intolerant of any other opinion. To me, the VIth Arrondissement has always represented the intellectual and artistic pulse of the city. The Sorbonne, the Ecole des Beaux Arts – these seats of learning symbolized freedom of thought, the exchange of ideas and ideologies.

This didn't discourage us from finding another vantage point for our cameras. Across the street, near the Café des Beaux Arts, we spotted a suitable third-floor window. The woman who lived in the apartment was Italian, and she couldn't have been more pleasant to us. Even though this was the opening day of an art show she was exhibiting there, she told us we were welcome to use her window. Then she saw our equipment – the cameras, the lights, the cables, not to mention the number of people involved – and expressed great concern that all this extra weight would cause the floor to collapse and we would end up in the apartment below. So we took the minimum we needed to take a few shots, and before I left I bought one of the paintings.

In the middle of all this first-day mayhem I was approached by a stranger in the street who asked if we needed the use of a garden for our film. The man casually making this generous offer was the theatre director Alfredo Arias, who just happened to be passing by. We still hadn't found a garden so we were excited by what seemed like an unexpected solution to our problem. When you are making a film on location people often come and offer you things but, unfortunately, they are not always suitable. And so, alas, it was in this case when we realized Mr Arias' garden was too small for our needs.

*   *   *

Shortly after shooting began I had to pack up and move out of my apartment to allow the art department to prepare it for the film. There was a certain irony in this. For thirty-five years I have used every kind of cajolery to get people out of their homes if those homes afford the perfect location for our films. But as Madeleine Castaing's apartment had inspired *The Proprietor*, the film would inevitably be shot there and I would have to move to a hotel.

I began to have some sympathy for the people whose homes we have invaded in the past. Not only did I have to move out, but I also had to watch my new home being stripped and put through three extensive transformations: the apartment as it was when Adrienne was a child; the empty, dilapidated shell she comes to buy; and her subsequent refurbishment – even, in one scene, Adrienne smashing a hammer through the plaster of a wall. The up-side was that certain essential renovations were done to the apartment under the aegis of the production – the ancient parquet floors, for example, which were broken in places needed to be repaired and levelled in order for the camera to move fluidly.

Only Jeanne, Marc and I knew the full history of the apartment and its significance to the film. The crew, the technicians, the rest of the cast came and went doing their work, unaware of the role the apartment had played and continued to play in this enterprise.

We had established as our base the Académie des Beaux Arts, where we were allowed to park our vehicles and also to erect a marquee in the courtyard where the cast and crew would have their lunch. It is very rare for a film unit to be based in such beautiful surroundings, or enjoy such extremely good lunches – though one might expect it in France. Important visitors frequently came to see us on the set, including Monsieur Douste-Blazy, the Minister of Culture, whom I had last encountered so dramatically on the steps of the Palais du Festival at Cannes.

When Monsieur Baldelli, the special adviser to cinema at the Ministry of Culture, came to visit I took him to lunch at the Café des Beaux Arts and, coincidentally, we were seated at the same table that Jeanne, Marc and I had occupied on the night Jeanne first came to see the apartment. That was the night the seed of this film began to germinate, and now, less than a year later, it was sprouting. That dinner with Jeanne and Marc had been, in a way, a celebration of things to come, even though at that time I had no idea of what they might be.

I celebrate my intentions in advance of their happening because it's a way of focusing the force of my will like a laser beam to make these things happen. And yet it still surprises me when they do . . .

A few days before we were scheduled to shoot the sequence in Elliott Spencer's garden we still hadn't found the appropriate location, so tracking down a garden now became a matter of urgency. Once again Pamela Ballweg came to our rescue. She knew of a garden attached to an eighteenth-century house on rue de l'Université. As I was in the middle of shooting I asked Marc to go and see it, and he reported back that it was ideal but rather unkempt, and the few existing plants had deteriorated in the heat wave that was currently suffocating the whole of Paris.

Marc suggested we should go to the flower market on the Île de la Cité and restock. So during the lunch break one of the props men took Marc and me in a unit truck to the Île de la Cité, where we loaded up with lavender, hortensias and hibicus. Then Marc worked all afternoon getting the garden ready.

Because of the urgency with which we had to acquire this location we were in no position to negotiate with the owner who demanded the excessive sum of twenty-five thousand francs. What concerned me more was that we had only two days to shoot twelve pages of the screenplay – the difficult scenes where Adrienne meets Elliott, Franz and Patrice again after a separation of thirty years. Attempting to do such subtle and moving scenes, requiring so much from the actors, in such a short space of time was madness. But time, as we soon discovered, was the least of our problems.

By then, the heat wave which had settled over the whole of Europe that summer was at its height. Larry had erected a silk screen over the garden to diffuse the light, but this also had the effect of trapping the hot static air like a greenhouse, making the conditions even more unbearable. At one point it became so intensely hot that Jeanne almost passed out. Her make-up was running, her clothes were sticking to her, she was in such discomfort I feared she might have a heart attack. The thermometer read 114 degrees. I went in search of the owner of the house to ask if he could open the door from the garden into the living room so that overheated cast and crew members might sit and cool down. At first I couldn't find him, and when I did he was rather abrupt and said that his son had the key. So we went to look for the son who told us that his father had the key. Apparently, father and son had quarrelled that day and weren't speaking to each other, and seemed to be taking it out on us. Finally, we located the mother who came down from some cool part of the house and allowed Jeanne, but only Jeanne, access to the living room.

At the end of our second night, when shooting was over, I arranged with the Indian restaurant Vishnu to deliver a wonderful dinner for the unit who had worked so hard in such demanding circumstances. That, and lots of icy Veuve Clicquot were set out on a table in the courtyard – and the first people to rush to the table were the owner of the house, his wife and son.

The film sequences of the 1960s and 1970s – those scenes that everyone had cautioned me about – worked out better than anyone had expected. For the 1960s film we had found some young French actors who brought the right quality of the New Wave to their performance – capturing something of the cool detachment and ambiguity of films like Malle's *The Lovers* and *Lift to the Scaffold* or Truffaut's *Four Hundred Blows*. Making a contrastingly garish and glamorous 1970s version of that film was also very interesting for me because at that time I was producing the kind of films that had no place in mainstream cinema, and now here was an opportunity to film a scene in the popular Hollywood style of the period.

The property auction, which had so fascinated me months earlier, was incorporated into the script, and we reproduced the exact ritual in the film. At the beginning of the proceedings a single candle is lit by the magistrates and burns throughout the auction. When the bidding on a lot ceases, a second candle is lit from the flame of the first. The smaller candle extinguishes automatically after two minutes, and if there are no further bids during this period the lot goes to the last bidder. If, however, bidding recommences, the second candle is extinguished until the bidding ceases again, when a third candle is lit. The last bid made before that candle burns out is accepted as final. Unsuccessful bidders (as Adrienne was) then have ten days to come up with another offer on the lot which needs to exceed the final bid by at least ten per cent. Then they return, make their counter-offer, and wait while the candle dies out.

We were given permission to shoot these scenes at the Chambre de Notaire at Châtelet. But it wasn't just the Chambre de Notaire I wanted – I also wanted to use the real auctioneers and magistrates and, intrigued by this proposal, they agreed to take part. We were only allowed access for two days, but we managed to finish this difficult and technically complex sequence within that time.

By the time we came to do this scene Charlotte de Turckheim was in Canada working on another film. But like everyone else involved, Charlotte was so committed to this project that she agreed to fly back overnight; she arrived on set straight from the airport at seven the next morning and worked all through the day. She was, quite simply, amazing. When we finished, the President of the Chambre de Notaire invited us all for a drink in his wood-panelled office hung with portraits of grand judges who had presided over the activities of this place in the past.

The heat wave broke, albeit for only forty-eight hours, on the very day we needed shimmering blue skies for the scenes in the penthouse of the Sony building. These were critical scenes between Virginia Kelly and Patrice, and Virginia Kelly and Adrienne – commerce versus art. I had planned to shoot much of those sequences outside on the terrace and take advantage of the panoramic view – the height of this penthouse as a kind of metaphor of Virginia Kelly's stature in her profession. But that morning the sky was a gloomy gun-metal grey, and soon great sheets of rain were lashing the plate-glass walls of the boardroom.

We were told the rain would eventually clear. However, we couldn't waste the morning so Larry set up his lights on the terrace and flooded the boardroom with synthetic sunshine so we could, at least, shoot some of the indoor scenes. By lunchtime there was no sign that the rain was letting up and with nothing more we could shoot at the Sony building that day, we moved the unit to the next location – the Hôpital de la Pitié Salpêtrière, where Franz Legendre is recovering from his illness.

The sudden change of plans meant that my assistant, Christopher Granier-Deferre, had no time to assemble the extras we needed for the hospital scene. Christopher – the son of English actress Susan Hampshire and French director Pierre Granier-Deferre – had been a great asset when he worked with us on *Jefferson*, not only usefully bilingual but also very resourceful. So he hastily improvised – putting some of the crew members into white coats, hanging stethoscopes around their necks, and hoping they would pass as doctors.

As the heat of the city became more and more unbearable Jeanne decided to spend her weekends in Versailles, in the relative coolness of the air-conditioned Trianon Palace Hotel. One weekend it was necessary for Josh Hamilton to read through the New York section of the script with Jeanne, so Josh and I, together with Andy Litvack and my nephew Rizwan, who was visiting me in Paris, went to Versailles. We worked with Jeanne in her suite which overlooked a delightful meadow with a weeping willow at its centre and sheep grazing all around. In the late afternoon light the meadow appeared particularly ethereal, and we all went for a long walk around it. I felt that this setting would make a far better location for the last scene of the film than the one we had planned – a hotel in the middle of Paris. The beauty and tranquillity of this place would represent the peace Adrienne had finally found.

Humbert Balsan tried to organize this, but he was told that at the time we wanted to shoot, one wing of the hotel would be closed for renovation and the other wing had already been reserved by a football team. I asked Jeanne to speak with the people at the hotel to see if there was anything she could do, but the response was exactly the same. My colleagues all told me to face the fact that this time I was *not* going to find the perfect location and to stop wasting time and get on with finding a place in Paris. It was practical advice, of course, but I wouldn't give up without one final shot. I asked my assistant to send a fax to the hotel asking for a suite for the Maharaja of Jodhpur. If this scheme didn't work, then I would take it as a sign that we were not meant to shoot here, and I would look for another location. But we received a fax confirming the reservation for the Maharaja of Jodhpur. When I told Jeanne what I had done she roared with laughter and told me I was completely crazy.

Of course now that the hotel was expecting the Maharaja of Jodhpur there was no way we could shoot the film except under cover. The scenario I came up with, should anyone at the hotel ask, was that the Maharaja of Jodhpur was to be interviewed by Jeanne Moreau for French television. This was an extraordinary situation: film-makers playing the parts of royalty in order to make a film.

On the day in question I dressed in an elegant silk kurta and pyjama and, assuming my most imperious manner, arrived at the Trianon Palace Hotel at seven in the morning looking every inch the Maharaja of Jodhpur. I was accompanied by my cameraman Larry, dressed in a smart white suit. With his wavy silver locks and Spanish grandee descent he looked absolutely right in the part of the Maharaja's private secretary. Humbert, wearing a dark suit, dark glasses and a menacing expression, performed brilliantly as the Maharaja's bodyguard. As I led my entourage into the hotel everyone bowed to us and addressed me as 'Your Highness'.

The assistant manager showed us into a magnificent suite which, much to my consternation, did not overlook the meadow. I walked on to the balcony and surveyed a splendid view of rooftops and television aerials. 'No,' I said to the assistant manager. 'This is not a suite the Maharaja likes.' He looked crestfallen as he explained that it was the best suite in the entire hotel. 'The Maharaja,' I said, 'would like a view of the meadow.'

The meadow, replied the assistant manager apologetically, could only be seen from the other wing which was presently closed for renovation. Nevertheless the Maharaja insisted on having a view of the meadow and the assistant manager had no option but to comply.

We were taken to the suite that Jeanne had previously occupied, and indeed it was in a terrible state. The furniture was piled up in one corner, plastic sheeting covered the floor, the electric sockets had been removed, and so had all the bathroom fittings. 'This suite,' I announced, 'is very much to the Maharaja's taste.' The assistant manager looked very surprised by this and expressed great concern that the Maharaja would be most uncomfortable, unable even to take a bath or shower. I told him that was of no importance, Maharajas do not take showers or baths – the Maharaja's lackeys would bring buckets of water to the balcony and bathe the Maharaja; that is how Maharajas bathed in India. He was clearly very alarmed by this information, but he was in no position to argue with the Maharaja of Jodhpur.

By then Jeanne had arrived and been put into the suite we had originally been shown, and where she and Charlotte were to be made-up and dressed. Flowers, fruit, huge trays of sweets, breakfast, everything you can imagine was sent up to Jeanne with the compliments of the hotel.

In order not to arouse any suspicion about our real purpose we had arranged for only the barest equipment and the minimum of crew, and two by two they stealthily made their way into the hotel. The builders were fascinated by all these comings and goings in the dismantled suite and, worried that their noise would disturb us, voluntarily stopped working and left.

When the deputy director of the hotel and her assistant, two very courteous but formidable ladies, heard that we were setting up cameras and lights in the suite, they sent a message telling us to stop. I asked Jeanne to speak with the deputy director and her assistant, and a meeting was called in the lobby where Jeanne and I tried to convince the two formidable ladies that they should allow the interview to proceed as planned. After a great deal of discussion – presenting our arguments and listening to their objections – they gave us permission to shoot the 'interview'.

In public everyone addressed me as 'Your Highness', and when Larry, Humbert, Charlotte and I went to lunch in the pretty terrace restaurant overlooking the garden, Charlotte decided that as I had not given her a role to play in this masquerade she would take it upon herself to play the part of the Maharaja's concubine, and she became very coquettish. The Maharaja of Jodhpur is a

51

good friend of mine and if it ever came to his attention that I had assumed his identity, I know he would just laugh and think 'Oh, it's just Ismail up to his tricks again'. But I wasn't sure how he might react if he were to read in *France-Soir* an account of his 'tryst' at the Trianon Palace Hotel with the French actress Charlotte de Turckheim.

Earlier that morning I had noticed the hotel's ballroom and decided to film one last shot there, but I didn't tell the formidable ladies of the hotel about this until after we had finished shooting in the suite. Then the ladies were summoned and told of our intention to use the ballroom for part of the 'interview'. They explained that the ballroom had been prepared for a conference at eight o'clock, but by now they realized there was no point in arguing with us and gave their permission. We moved the conference table to one side, shot the necessary footage of Jeanne and Charlotte, replaced the table, and the Maharaja and his entourage swept majestically out of the hotel at exactly eight o'clock.

The Maharaja, however, might just as well have remained in Jodhpur. For when we came to edit the film I had another change of heart – not untypical in movie-making – and decided on an entirely different location for the final scene of the film. The interior *is* the one we shot at the Trianon Palace, but the view from the window is not that of the meadow we had gone to such duplicitous lengths to acquire, but a seascape we had shot earlier at Cannes.

We had been looking for an unusual château to shoot the scene where Patrice Legendre and Virginia Kelly fall in love, but none of the ones we saw fitted my visual concept for that scene. Humbert asked the distinguished French historian Hervé Gransart, who had worked with us on *Jefferson in Paris*, for some suggestions and Hervé came up with the seventeenth-century Château Villette at Vigny in the Val d'Oise some forty kilometres from Paris. This was the last mansion to be built by the French classical architect François Mansart. It was commissioned by Jean Dyel II, Louis XIII's ambassador to Venice, who wanted the château designed in the style of the Italian villa he had inhabited in the Veneto.

Hervé warned us that access to the property had always been denied to film-makers in the past, and that it would probably be impossible to shoot there unless we had some connection with the present owners. By another of those inexplicable coincidences that brought all the elements of this film together, Humbert told us that his father and the owner of the château were cousins, and he remembered going to a family wedding there some thirty years ago.

Humbert contacted Olivier Gerard, the son of the owner, whom he knew, but Olivier simply confirmed what we had been told by Hervé – that his parents never allowed filming at the château. Nevertheless, Humbert made arrangements for Larry, Marc and me to go and see the place, and while we were there Humbert spoke to his relatives and explained what we wanted to do. They remembered his father well, and through this family connection we were allowed to shoot at the château.

The Château Villette exceeded all my expectations as the location for this scene. The house and garden were glorious, but the centre of attraction was a marble fountain of Neptune sending cascades of water tumbling down a broad expanse of shallow stone steps – exactly like the thousand rills gushing down the terraces of the Villa d'Este in Italy, but on a miniature scale. The water system operated on remote control, and this facility inspired one of the most enchanting scenes in the film. When Patrice and Virginia come upon the fountain it is inactive, but at the moment they become aware of their feelings for each other and kiss, the fountain comes to life driving ripples of water into an ever-swelling flood down the steps and sending jets of water high into the sky. When I saw these possibilities and explained what I had in mind for the scene everybody expressed reservations that it would be corny. We would see.

Because the location itself was so idyllic I wanted the music for this scene to be romantic but not sentimental. George Trow had recommended the song 'If I didn't care' from the Inkspots, which is a love song with a lyrical lightness to it, and we hastily arranged for Marc to record it overnight before shooting the next day.

We had a number of scenes to shoot at the château, including a scene in which Patrice and Virginia encounter a wedding being held at the château. This involved one hundred and fifty extras, with very little time available as usual. But the golden light in the garden and over the lake was so beautiful we decided to do some additional shots of different vistas from various angles as advance punctuation to introduce the scenes of the château.

In the middle of the afternoon the whole place suddenly glowed in a unique golden-orange light, and the garden shimmered as though it had been sprinkled with gold dust. This is the kind of light cameramen can only dream about, and I knew we had to shoot the fountain scene immediately. There was no time for Marc and Sean to rehearse – they were quite surprised by this as the scene involved dialogue, singing, choreography, and absolute timing, and a rehearsal would normally be essential. Actors always feel they are rushed into things, but sometimes there are elements out of our control that we have to take advantage of, and nature had provided us with something quite magical that we could never have reproduced artificially. When we came to watch the rushes, everyone agreed I had been right, and even Jim conceded that this scene was actually very charming and light-hearted.

Our last day of shooting at Château Villette was also the last day of shooting in France, so that night we gave a party for the French cast and crew on the grounds of the château where we had erected a huge marquee. The marquee was full of iced champagne, Indian food, and about one hundred and fifty exhausted, happy people. Jeanne had not been involved in the scenes at the château, so I was delighted that she came all the way from Paris for the party, despite the fact that she was leaving for New York the next day.

We have a tradition at Merchant Ivory that everyone who works on our films receives a gift on the last night. This is not only something to remind them of their experience of working with us, but also a gesture of gratitude for their hard work. This time, the present was silk Nehru jackets which I had ordered from Bombay – and everyone was delighted by the gift.

*   *   *

3

4

7

8

9

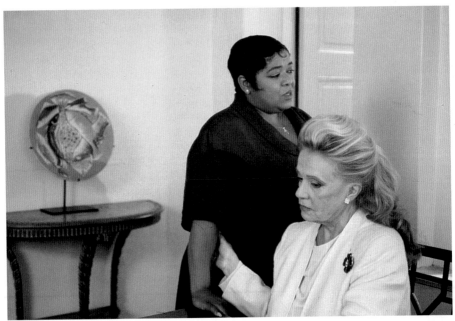

10

12

13

15

16

18

19

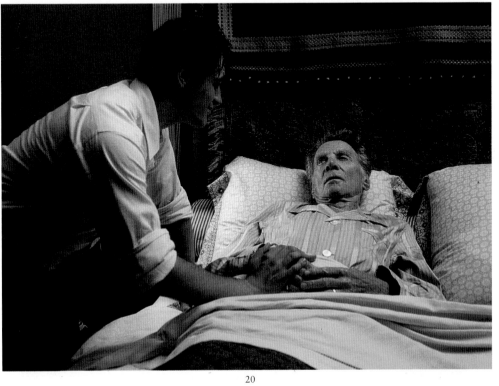

20

21

22

While I had been busy on *The Proprietor*, pre-production work was also progressing on *Surviving Picasso*. But only two months before shooting was due to start we faced an unexpected development. Claude Picasso, Pablo Picasso's son, and Françoise Gilot, Claude's mother, who had previously agreed to co-operate with us, suddenly withdrew their consent, claiming that we were breaching both copyright and privacy laws. Nevertheless, we decided to go ahead with the film – which we had every right to do. But given Picasso's and Gilot's objections, we suspected they might try to stop the shooting. In order to avoid troublesome and costly interruptions during filming, therefore, we felt it would be prudent to maintain a low profile on this project by shooting the film covertly at undisclosed locations in the South of France and England.

There were two scenes in the film, however, that there was no discreet way of shooting and would have exposed us completely – the Occupation of Paris by the Nazis, and the subsequent Liberation by the Allies. We had intended to shoot these scenes at Place de la Concorde and now there was a serious risk that, if we did, the gendarmes would come and stop us.

By coincidence, there was also an Occupation scene in *The Proprietor*, and this gave us an idea of how we could solve our other dilemma. Of all the extraordinary things I have done in the course of my career I have never before shot two films simultaneously – but that is exactly what we were planning to do now. Under cover of shooting the war scenes for *The Proprietor* we would, at the same time, be shooting them for *Surviving Picasso* – and neither Gilot nor Picasso would be aware of it and, therefore, able to stop it.

At six o'clock on the morning of Sunday, 20 August 1995 – the last opportunity to shoot this scene in the relatively deserted city before the Parisians returned from their vacations – we arrived in Place de la Concorde with three cameras, a huge crew, hundreds of extras, period cars – the works. Of course, if you move into Place de la Concorde on such a scale, every television station and newspaper from every corner of the world comes to see what's going on. Even Jeanne called me from New York the next day to tell me that Merchant Ivory's Occupation of Paris was all over American television. Naturally we told all the reporters that we were shooting scenes for *The Proprietor*, which was the truth – though not the whole truth. Nobody could ever have guessed that we were shooting two completely separate films. It was an absolute triumph.

Just how authentic these scenes looked can be judged by the reaction of a young American couple staying at the Crillon, the grand hotel which overlooks Place de la Concorde. In Paris on their honeymoon, they woke up to the startling sight of thousands of soldiers, marching bands and tanks massed in the square. They packed their bags in a panic, ready to take the next plane back to the States, until the concierge at the Crillon told them that Paris was, indeed, under siege – but only by a film company.

Our caterers had laid out breakfast in the middle of Place de la Concorde, and I was joined there by Marc and my friend Bettina Graziani, once a famous *haute couture* model and now a supporter of the arts and benefactress of young people. I remembered that as a college student in Bombay I had a private fantasy that some day I would go to Paris and study French at the Sorbonne. It was an odd dream to have because I had only ever seen pictures of Paris in books – there was no television, nor any French films in India then. As things turned out, I went to New York not Paris to study, but now at the age of fifty-eight my dream was finally realized – though I never imagined that when I did eventually come to this city I would be occupying it in such a manner. Not only did I have an apartment in Paris but, for this day at least, I owned it – from the Madeleine to the Assemblée Nationale. And just to complete the dream, I intend to enrol for the winter semester at the Sorbonne to study French.

CHANGING PLACES: THREE WEEKS IN NEW YORK

The following morning, Monday, 21 August, Larry Pizer and I took the Concorde to New York. Extravagant, perhaps, but we had only twenty-four hours before we commenced work there. On a previous visit I had organized the locations, and cast all the roles except for some minor ones. The New York shoot seemed to be under control, with no foreseeable problems. Hubris.

For the part of Adrienne's housekeeper, Milly, I had set my heart on the Broadway star Nell Carter. I have been a great admirer of hers since I saw her in the musical *Ain't Misbehavin'* on Broadway in 1979 and, in fact, had offered her the part of the nightclub singer in our first French film *Quartet*, which she was unable to do as the dates clashed with a big television series. Nevertheless, we had kept in touch over the years, and when I contacted her and said I wanted her to play opposite Jeanne Moreau in a film I was directing she thought I was pulling her leg, until I convinced her that I was serious.

In the role of Willy Kunst, Adrienne's literary agent who urges her to return to Paris, we cast Austin Pendleton with whom we had worked on *Mr and Mrs Bridge* and *The Ballad of the Sad Café*.

Sam Waterston agreed to play the role of Harry Bancroft, the antique dealer from Christie's to whom Adrienne sells her collection before leaving New York. Sam had worked with us on *Savages* in 1972, and has done great work in films like *The Great Gatsby*, *The Killing Fields* (for which he won an Oscar nomination for Best Actor), and Woody Allen's *Hannah and her Sisters* and *Crimes and Misdemeanors*.

Christopher Reeve, an old friend and a veteran of two Merchant Ivory films, *The Bostonians* and *The Remains of the Day*, had originally accepted that part. We were all devastated when we heard the news of his riding accident, and that this fine actor had been struck such a cruel blow. How helpless we are in these circumstances, beyond offering our prayers, our encouragement and support. But Christopher is a fighter, and if anyone has the strength and the courage to overcome this, it is he.

On Tuesday we had a read-through of the script at the Plaza Hotel where we had taken a conference room. Then I went to see Barbara Ziegler, the scion of a distinguished American family, who had agreed to let us use her apartment on East 66th Street as the location for Adrienne's New York home. Barbara has lived in this apartment for nearly thirty years and has created a warm and comfortable environment of books, paintings and objects that are cherished – valued, rather than just being valuable – which suited Adrienne's style.

We began shooting there early the next morning, with only a minor setback when the industrial-strength hairdryer being used on Nell Carter's hair blew every fuse in the apartment. But that was nothing compared to the shock we received that afternoon when a letter was delivered to us from the management company of the building ordering us to leave. Before we even had time to digest this news another letter arrived, this time from the lawyers of the co-op board stating that non-residential activity in the building was forbidden without the board's permission – and they weren't giving it. Barbara was furious. We were able to do one scene as planned, but had no clue what our next move would be.

Finding a location the day before shooting, as we had often had to do in Paris, is one thing: finding a substitute location for a place where you've already begun shooting is quite another. To inter-rupt a finely-timed schedule in order to search for another location while time runs out is a film-maker's nightmare.

Donald Rosenfeld and I immediately started to call anyone who might be able to intercede with the co-op board so that we could continue shooting in the building. We called the Mayor's office, every senator we knew, lawyers – even Patricia Scott Read, the Commissioner of Film, Theatre and Broadcasting (she received our call while lying on the dentist's couch, and leapt out of the surgery in the middle of her treatment to come to our aid).

While efforts were being made on our behalf, we decided to return to the building the following day and risk shooting some footage. When I arrived Nell Carter was waiting outside, and she pointed out the window of the board president's apartment. Winking at me, she went and stood on the pavement directly beneath the board president's window and suddenly belted out the song 'There's No Business Like Show Business' – her huge voice ringing out as far as Staten Island. When the laughter and applause of the assembled crowd died down, Nell and I walked into the building where we were stopped by the doorman who told us we would have to use the service entrance. We were in dispute with the board though a misunderstanding, but that was no reason to make us travel in the service elevator.

The doorman did, however, allow Jeanne to use the main entrance because he recognized her from an interview she had given on the television programme *60 Minutes*. 'Can you imagine that,' Jeanne said to me when we had reconvened in the apartment. 'Because I have been seen on *60 Minutes* I am considered a reliable person. You spend your whole life making films but you're remembered from an interview on *60 Minutes*.'

We were losing time, we were losing money, but we never lost heart. By now the story had hit the press, and we had dozens of calls from people offering us their homes for the film. It seems that for all the mean-spirited people in the world there are just as many good-spirited ones. The *New York Times* ran a story on the incident, and when they asked me for my reaction I told them that my father used to say that when one door shuts a hundred others will open.

Shooting could not be held up, so while we were trying to sort out the problems of the apartment we also had to rearrange our entire schedule in order not to waste any more of our precious shooting time. We had to reorganize our other locations and reapply for permissions, cast actors, give notice to the Mayor's office and the police – all the arrangements we had made months earlier now had to be done again.

Christopher Mason, Barbara Ziegler's godson, suggested we should take a look at a town house just across the street from Barbara's apartment, and I asked Donald to go and see it while I went to begin work in Harlem with Sam Waterston and Nell and her screen family. This premature removal to shoot the scenes at milly's apartment had been forced on us by the recent developments, and the art department had their work cut out to get the Harlem locations prepared immediately. Nevertheless, the crew packed the equipment, loaded their trucks, and we moved to Harlem with renewed spirit.

We hadn't yet cast the parts of Milly's husband and child. I saw two actors for the part of the husband, but the one I chose immediately complained that the part was too small. Nevertheless he agreed to do it – then one hour before shooting he completely disappeared. We managed to find a replacement at the last moment, but by then our nerves had become quite frayed. To add to our troubles we discovered that the child we had cast was camera-shy and very self-conscious: Nell had to spend a long time trying to make him relax and overcome his shyness. It had been a long, long day. And it wasn't over yet.

Donald reported that the town house, which belonged to Dr Joseph Santo who owns The Sign of the Dove restaurant in New York, could be a good substitute. As it was going to be rented out it was unfurnished and therefore gave us an opportunity of recreating something of Barbara Ziegler's apartment, plus scope to realize some other ideas which would not have been possible before. Late that night I took the art director and his crew to the house to see if it would be possible to paint, decorate and furnish the place in forty-eight hours.

Dr Santos' brother, a part-owner of the house, wasn't very keen to let us use it. But I think Dr Santos' secretary, Leonore, picked up our sense of urgency and desperation and told Dr Santos that she would be very disappointed if he refused because Nell Carter was her favourite singer. She also reminded him that his young nephew had ambitions to work in the movies, and when we agreed to allow the young man on the set the deal was settled.

Barbara was magnificent. She offered us whatever of her paintings, furniture and objects we needed to prepare our new set, and over the weekend her possessions were shifted from one side of the street to the other, where the art department were working like Trojans to transform Dr Santos' house into Adrienne's apartment.

During this upheaval we managed to shoot our scenes in Central Park and at Christie's, the auctioneers. We still needed a few special pieces for Adrienne's set, so during a lunch break from the Christie's shoot Donald Rosenfeld and I went to look at antique shops on 2nd Avenue. There was one particular shop I hadn't visited in some ten years, and when I greeted the lady who runs it and asked if I might borrow some pieces for a film I was making she looked surprised. I introduced myself, and explained that we hadn't seen each other in a long time. She asked me to jog her memory about when we had last met. She was very polite, but clearly didn't remember me, so – as I selected the various pieces which were suitable for the set – I told her that I was the producer of *A Room With a View*, *Howards End* and *The Remains of the Day*. 'Oh,' she said, 'you are a very distinguished producer.' And she allowed me to pick out eight of her most valuable pieces.

The art department worked away like beavers preparing the two sets – Dr Santos' house and Harlem – simultaneously. They rushed about in every direction – their three vans speeding between prop houses in the Bronx and downtown Manhattan and the two locations in mid-town Manhattan and Upper Harlem, unloading furniture at lightning speed before screeching off again. We even managed to get a flashing light and siren for one of the vans so that it could cut through the notorious traffic jams just like the undercover police cars in the movies. Even the Teamsters, the truck drivers who make up the biggest and most powerful trade union in America, got caught up in all this activity. The Teamsters are popularly perceived as idlers, sitting by their trucks playing cards instead of doing any work. I think this may have been the first time that the Teamsters rolled up their sleeves and got into the act.

Our trucks and generators were still parked in Barbara's street on the opposite side of the road, but as we were no longer shooting in her building there was nothing her co-op board could do about it – except stare at us disapprovingly whenever they passed our trucks.

Our new location was, in many ways, better than our original one. As well as an impressive study with a wood-burning fireplace, the house had a small garden, and a balcony overlooking a patio. The only disadvantage was that as a private house it lacked the awninged entrance of an apartment building, where we also had scenes to shoot. Opposite the house was an apartment building with a smart entrance which would suit us very well. But after our experience at Barbara Ziegler's building we were hesitant about getting involved in any more unpleasantness. Well, we would lose nothing by asking – and we were very relieved when the board of *that* building said they were looking forward to our visit.

While we were filming these exterior shots the art department came to me with the news that our next location, Raoul's restaurant in SoHo, wasn't ready for shooting. We had fixed this location months earlier, and although the restaurant was undergoing renovations we had been assured that the work would be completed by the time we came to shoot. However, it was far from ready. We started looking for a substitute and found the Odeon in Tribeca which actually suited us better than Raoul's. Where Raoul's was divided in two by the centrally placed kitchen, the Odeon had its kitchen to one side, leaving a huge space where we could move our cameras without any restrictions.

There was a similar change of plans just before we came to film at Geoffrey Beene's store on Fifth Avenue. The fashion designer had previously agreed to the shooting then suddenly changed his mind. Apparently he felt that the film did not correspond with the image his clothes projected. I simply couldn't believe this. I contacted Dawn Mello at Bergdorf Goodman, the classiest, most stylish, most exclusive store in New York where the top names of *haute couture* – from Chanel to Versace – are presented in coolly elegant surroundings, and we were told that Merchant Ivory could certainly shoot there. This was, again, a better location for us geographically in that when Adrienne leaves the Edwardian Room at the Plaza Hotel she would automatically come upon Berfdorf Goodman, which is the adjacent building. Each of these enforced changes seemed to indicate that somebody up there was looking after our interests; the places we had originally found didn't suit us nearly as much as the ones we ended up using in the film.

Shooting was interrupted by Labor Day, which is a national holiday in America, and Jeanne came with her son Jerome to spend that weekend with us at our house in upstate New York. A relaxing weekend walking around the pond, listening to music and reading was just what we needed . . .

We had now been evicted from three of our pre-arranged locations in New York. You could say a pattern was emerging. So when we were evicted from our fourth, the Museum of Modern Art, it didn't come as such a great surprise – although the circumstances caused me a great deal of disappointment. Merchant Ivory have been great supporters of the museum for over thirty years; we have exhibited our films for them, given benefits, made donations – we have never ignored any of their appeals to us. Now, after agreeing to let us shoot there, they were demanding substantial fees for this privilege. Part of the function of such institutions, after all, is to help promote the arts, which are always in a struggle for survival. But, instead of that, they were making impossible demands on the very people they should have been assisting.

The Museum of Modern Art had an installation of video art by the enigmatic, exploratory French film-maker Chris Marker. A former poet, novelist, critic and collaborator of Resnais, Marker's intensely personal films are almost an extension of his literary inclinations – essays worked on celluloid rather than paper. The opening scene of *The Proprietor* is set in an art gallery, and I thought this exhibition of Marker's art would work well for our film. By now it was almost predictable that we would find a connection with Chris Marker. His producer, Françoise Widoff, was a friend of Humbert's. So when we had to transfer shooting to the Gagosian Gallery in SoHo, it was a simple matter to arrange for Marker's installation to come with us.

In a tight three-week shoot we had had to find and organize substitutes for four of our six locations, and we still managed to bring the film in on time and within budget. To a large degree this was achieved by an incredibly committed and focused cast and crew who never gave less than a hundred per cent.

We had another shot to do of Jeanne walking in Central Park – a tiny figure against this great landscape – and we decided to shoot in the area known as the Sheep Meadow. We arrived very early in the morning amid some chaos because not everyone was quite sure of where exactly we were shooting, and things were a little mixed up.

In order to get a sense of scale, I wanted to film this shot from a height – but we didn't have any scaffolding or platform. By another of those uncanny coincidences that I had become used to by now, the Sheep Meadow was also a location for the new $50 million plus Schwarzenegger movie *Eraser*. I noticed that standing by the entrance of their set – a very elaborate one which was in the process of being built – there were two wheeled scaffolds. How convenient, I thought – and suggested to my crew that we should borrow one. It was still very early and the crew constructing the Schwarzenegger set hadn't yet arrived, so we just helped ourselves to one of their scaffolds, wheeling it over to our part of the meadow.

Larry was on the scaffold with the camera taking shots of the rooftops and buildings around the park when Schwarzenegger's crew arrived and noticed that one of their scaffolds was missing. Of course the culprits were immediately evident, so they marched over to us, irate that we had stolen their equipment. I introduced myself, but it was clear from their attitude that they perceived me as some light-fingered fly-by-night character, and demanded to know if our crew were union members. Union crews can be very officious about their status, and make things very sticky for non-union films. The union demands a minimum scale of fees for its members, which many small independent films can't afford. Often they picket non-union films as a way of disrupting shooting or recruiting members. Our union members – the grip and the electrician – hadn't arrived yet because of the confusion over the location so, as we couldn't produce them, we were told we would be reported to the union.

We tried to plead that our poverty-stricken, low-budget cir-cumstances had reduced us to the unauthorized appropriation of their equipment. But this cut no ice with Schwarzenegger's men. I remembered that the Schwarzenegger film was being made by Warner's, so I told the other crew that we were also making a film for Warner's called *Surviving Picasso*, and that their location manager could call Bill Gerber, our executive at the Warner's studio, who could vouch for us.

While they went off to discuss this development, Jeanne arrived. I wanted her to be shot walking in the enclosed part of the meadow, but we discovered that the entrance was locked. Jeanne gamely volunteered to climb over the six-foot fence, and I was about to lift her over when everyone shouted at me to stop because there might be an accident and Jeanne could get hurt. Eventually we found a gardener who opened the entrance for us but would only allow one person inside the enclosure. Jeanne went in, and when the gardener had disappeared from sight my assistant and I scrambled over the fence, showed Jeanne which direction to go in, and scrambled out again.

We were shooting the scene when our union grip finally arrived. Unfortunately, he didn't have his union card with him and the Schwarzenegger crew began agitating again. While that was going on, we completed our shots, dismantled the camera, and quietly wheeled the scaffold back. Jeanne, meanwhile, discovered that she couldn't get out of the enclosure because the gardener had locked the gate and gone for his coffee break. We had no idea where to find him. We could not leave Jeanne permanently in Central Park so we approached our rich cousins, the Schwarzenegger team – who were now rather less hostile because of our Warner's connection – managed to borrow a ladder, and hoisted Jeanne over the fence.

Our final scene in New York was in the Edwardian Room at the Plaza Hotel. No film hd been shot in this room for over twenty years, and I wondered whether they would suddenly have a change of heart and turn us away. But the people at the Plaza were very co-operative and allowed us access from three in the afternoon until midnight.

We finally wrapped the film at 11 p.m. on 11 September. Exhausted, happy, triumphant.

Then we had a wonderful surprise. The chefs at the Plaza

invited some of us to their own dining room near the kitchens, where the Irish chef Joe Friel had prepared a splendid feast, served by the other chefs who all looked very impressive in their tall white toques. The following night we held a wrap party to mark the end of the American shoot, at Shaan, an Indian restaurant in mid-town Manhattan. Each member of the team was given a gift of a hand-woven cotton kurta, the loose Indian shirt, which I had ordered to be sent from Bombay. Everyone became very emotional because it's always sad when you finish a film and you must part from people you have grown close to over the months of working together.

After dinner George Trow made a wonderfully eloquent speech, and he ended it by turning to me and lifting his glass with the words 'To the greatest human being in the world'. Well, when someone pays you a tribute like that you can do one of two things – you can slide down the chair and hide under the table in embarrassment, or you can accept the compliment shamelessly. I chose the latter option, and leapt up from my chair. 'That's me!' I said.

It was such a good feeling to be surrounded by these warm people, each one of whom loved this film as much as I did. I thanked them all. And my first collaboration with Jeanne ended with a nod to future collaborations – until then, however, I hope we will continue to enjoy each other's friendship.

POSTSCRIPT OR PREVIEW . . .

The end of shooting is not, of course, the end of making the film. The material needs to be edited, the soundtrack must be added – there are still a thousand things to be done before it can be shown in the cinema. Our immediate priority, however, was to put together a short reel to present at MIFED, the annual film trade fair held in Milan at the beginning of November, where we hoped to attract buyers from territories which had not yet acquired distribution rights to the film. Although shooting for *Surviving Picasso* was due to start in the South of France on 25 September, I stole a few days in London to work with Humphrey Dixon, who has edited a number of our films including *A Room with a View*, and his associate William Webb.

Before Peter Elson took our promotional reel to MIFED, we arranged a screening in London, where many international distributors stop over on their way to Milan to attend even more screenings. Competition for the attendance of these buyers is so intense that it was something of a coup that Peter had managed to get a dozen of them to come and see our reel. When I arrived at the preview theatre, however, I discovered that their screening room was not equipped to run the double-headed reel; it could only run a married reel (where the magnetic sound and picture are mixed), and we had no married reel at that stage. I shot out of the theatre just as the buyers were arriving with Peter Elson. 'I'll be right back,' I yelled at an astonished Peter. 'I have to find another theatre.'

I ran from one screening room to another up and down Wardour Street begging for a fifteen-minute slot, but with all the MIFED buyers in town every screening room was booked solid from dawn to dusk. I went to see Nicole Mackie at Rank and fell on her mercy. Nicole runs Rank's International Department, but like every other preview theatre Rank's theatre was fully booked. However, because of our long association with Rank, Nicole arranged a fifteen-minute slot for us to be squeezed between the other screenings.

I sprinted back to the other preview theatre, adrenalin and pulse racing, collected Peter and the buyers and led them briskly through the streets of Soho like the Pied Piper of Hamelin, while my nephew Nayeem raced ahead to take the reel to the Rank projection room. A consequence of this sudden relocation which I had entirely overlooked was that, in addition to the dozen distributors who had come to watch our reel, there were over twenty other buyers already present for the scheduled screenings – and we now had a captive audience of some forty potential buyers. And those buyers who, but for these extraordinary circumstances, might never have seen our reel, now made offers for the film.

But the struggles of an independent film-maker don't end when the film is in the can, or even when it's finally playing in the cinema. In fact, the last chapter of this book is just the first chapter of a bigger and more incredible story; the story of how a film-maker has to fight to get his film distributed, exhibited and promoted, and then virtually has to become an assassin in order to get the money he is owed – and that's no exaggeration. One Italian distributor owed us thousands for *A Room with a View* but consistently refused to pay us until one day I turned up at his office with two neanderthal Indians and told him they were Indian mafia and we had come to collect. Actually they were two sword-bearing Sikh guards I had 'borrowed' from the Indian Embassy – but the Italian producer couldn't hand over our money fast enough.

Most of the time what begins on a film set with actors, crew and screenplay usually ends up in a courtroom with lawyers, judges and affidavits. And then there are the critics and audiences . . . One of the lessons I have learnt as a film-maker is that you can never predict how people will react to your films.

The time, the commitment, the energy you devote to a project – the somersaults and tricks you have to perform, the constant juggling, the diplomatic manoeuvres, the battles for finance – these are never taken into account by an audience or by the critics, nor is there any reason why they should be. None of that effort should be apparent in the finished product and, in the end, none of it matters except in so far as it produces what you set out to achieve. All that matters is whether people respond to the film,

68

whether it touches them in the way you intended. And that's why, despite the madness, we go on making movies.

I know that within the film industry I have a reputation as a financial wizard who can put together ambitious projects on tiny budgets by making the sort of deals no one else can make. Of course without that ability Merchant Ivory would never have been able to make the kind of films we've made: to find financing for films which for a very long time were perceived as having no commercial potential is an art in itself. But I hope that through *The Proprietor* people will see a more creative side to my art – an ability as a director to create real characters, to tell a story that means something and engages the audience emotionally. If I have achieved that, then this fairy story deserves to live 'happily ever after'.

SCREENPLAY

INTRODUCTION

The process by which a script becomes a film is a long and complex one. The writer's original draft will change and evolve as all the other elements of film-making come into play: the director's vision of the material, the actors cast, the locations chosen will all affect the shaping of subsequent drafts of the script. The final draft – or what screenwriters refer to with only a hint of bitterness as the *first* final draft – is really nothing of the kind. Once shooting starts the material will go through more changes. If an actor is unhappy with the lines or if a scene isn't working the dialogue will be tweaked, or even whole scenes rewritten. If shooting begins to run behind schedule entire scenes may be cut and the information contained in them worked in elsewhere. A change of location may necessitate certain changes in the script. One scene in *The Proprietor*, for example, was written for a location in an apartment in Paris, but as we were unable to find the right apartment we shifted the whole scene to a barge on the Seine.

Even when shooting is completed, more changes take place in the editing room. Some scenes will be removed from their original context and placed elsewhere in the film either for the sake of clarity or for dramatic effect. If the completed film is too long, scenes will be trimmed or cut out altogether.

This screenplay of *The Proprietor* is the original concept and does not correspond entirely with the finished film on the screen. I considered editing and rearranging it with that objective, but as this is a book about the making of a film, and as the discrepancy between script and screen is part of that process, it seemed more honest to leave it as it is.

Ismail Merchant
1996

SYNOPSIS

ADRIENNE MARK (JEANNE MOREAU) is 'one of the most famous women in the world'. In the 1960s she was one of a handful of men and women who redefined Western Culture. Of French nationality and Jewish descent, ADRIENNE was bravely modern. Her path led away from the past and into the future, she felt. Now, thirty years later, she finds that she does not understand the modern world she helped to invent. In our opening scene, ADRIENNE is attending an exhibit of video art at a SoHo gallery. Here is a manifestation of her dilemma; she has come to a 'cutting edge' exhibit, but finds the video installation by artist Chris Marker is about the mystery of the past. The most modern of modern artists is dealing with the issues she thought she had put behind her. To add to her confusion, she is approached by a young fan, WILLIAM O'HARA (JOSH HAMILTON), who approaches ADRIENNE because she is 'the real thing' and 'has all the answers' at exactly the moment when she wonders if she has any answers at all.

Over lunch, WILLY KUNST (AUSTIN PENDLETON) outlines ADRIENNE's situation, saying her time in America is over, her books no longer sell and no one is bidding for her services. It is time to go back to France. It is perhaps fate that there is another circumstance which impels ADRIENNE forward; her mother's apartment on Paris' Left Bank is about to be sold at auction. In this apartment occurred all the trauma of ADRIENNE's childhood – the events she hoped to have put behind her. From this apartment ADRIENNE's mother JUDITH was taken away by the SS during the Nazi occupation of Paris. Moreover, ADRIENNE has reason to believe that it was her mother's lover FAN FAN who turned JUDITH over to the Nazis. This auction allows ADRIENNE the opportunity to buy back her childhood home, and in owning it free and clear, she will at last become the proprietor of her own life. 'Buy your mother's apartment,' KUNST tells ADRIENNE. 'Go to Paris. Tell secrets.' 'I'll

75

have to uncover the secrets before I can tell them, Willy,'
ADRIENNE responds.

ADRIENNE's most important relationship in America is with her
housekeeper MILLY (NELL CARTER). MILLY understands
ADRIENNE, and gives her the courage to sell all her belongings, the evidence of her life in America, in order to buy her
mother's apartment. This process brings both women into contact
with HARRY BANCROFT (SAM WATERSTON), a haughty
representative of a New York auction house. The suspicion which
immediately develops between MILLY and BANCROFT sparks
an intense and comic relationship. Before leaving New York,
ADRIENNE gives MILLY a fine portrait of herself as a young
girl. This portrait was the one of ADRIENNE's possessions most
coveted by BANCROFT. In fact, he later visits MILLY and tries to
buy it from her at a reduced price. She rejects him.

WILLIAM O'HARA has been insistent in his pursuit of
ADRIENNE and she has resisted him, but she finally agrees to
meet for lunch. O'HARA is obsessed by the 'New Wave' film
which was made in the early 1960s from ADRIENNE's first and
most successful novel *Call Me French*. He is ashamed that he is at
work on a commercial project. 'Don't worry, Mr O'Hara,' she
tells him, 'we've all done things like that.' Shortly thereafter, she
leaves for France.

In Paris, ADRIENNE reconnects with a Paris which is very
much changed from the city she remembers, and with three old
friends: her ex-husband ELLIOTT SPENCER (CHRISTOPHER
CAZENOVE), an elegant Englishman with whom she spars in
conversation; RAYMOND (PIERRE VANECK), an old lover
who is as adoring as ever; and FRANZ LEGENDRE (JEAN-
PIERRE AUMONT), a legendary director of the 'New Wave'
period and an old friend. Immediately, a tour of her mother's
apartment is arranged; the apartment is almost unchanged. With
her on this tour are PATRICE LEGENDRE (MARC TISSOT)
who is FRANZ's son, and VIRGINIA KELLY (SEAN YOUNG).

PATRICE's relationship with VIRGINIA forms an important subplot of the film. VIRGINIA is a film executive of the modern type who wants to film a re-make of FRANZ LEGENDRE's most famous 'New Wave' film. PATRICE is in a difficult situation. He needs the money this project will raise for his aged father's care, but he is appalled at what VIRGINIA plans to do to the film. ADRIENNE's film, *Call Me French*, was 'remade' by Hollywood disastrously as reinforced by the abrasive words of WILLIAM O'HARA, 'Hollywood remakes suck.' So, PATRICE's relationship with VIRGINIA is on edge from the first moment we see them together, an important ingredient for the passion which follows.

The auction at which the apartment is put up for sale is a strange affair for ADRIENNE. The candle ritual used during bidding triggers a recurring nightmarish vision whereby ADRIENNE sees a birthday party held for her as a young girl. Her friends become accusers blaming ADRIENNE for the capturing of her mother by the Nazis. As she daydreams, RAYMOND and ELLIOTT are outbid and lose the apartment, but ADRIENNE has one more chance to raise additional monies to win the house. She immediately calls MILLY, her chief source of strength. She resolves to sell all her manuscripts to a rich TEXAN COUPLE in an attempt to raise the necessary cash. And when, in a melancholy mood, ADRIENNE walks alone to see her mother's apartment, she finds another surprise source of strength, WILLIAM O'HARA, ensconced there. 'Are you a ghost?' ADRIENNE asks. 'If I am, I'm a friendly one,' WILLIAM responds.

The money is still not enough and so in New York, MILLY secretly takes action. After some homework MILLY discovers the true value of the portrait of the young ADRIENNE MARK, and takes it to BANCROFT. He succumbs and this money enables ADRIENNE to buy the apartment at the second auction.

In New York, MILLY watches her television triumphantly as her famous friend ADRIENNE is honoured at a film festival surrounded by her 'new' family. Everything has been taken away from her and everything has been given back. MILLY looks at the place on her wall where the portrait had been, but it is not empty. In place of the portrait is a photograph of MILLY and ADRIENNE, a testimony to their friendship – the most valuable possession of all.

I would like *The Proprietor* to tell a new kind of truth about our 'multicultural' society. Each one of us brings something to it. We come from separate paths, from cultural traditions with deep roots which came out of the earth long ago and in very different places. Now, inevitably, we all live together. How shall we keep the *depth* of our very different traditions and live together harmoniously – and in truth? This is the question *The Proprietor* asks.

Ismail Merchant

Abbreviations

INT   interior
EXT   exterior

1 TITLE SEQUENCE.

Fade from black to: portrait of a naked man; babble of voices.
We are at the Museum of Modern Art; retrospective of the work
of an important artist of the 1960s. On the face of ADRIENNE
MARK. ADRIENNE *is a woman of astonishing beauty, more*
remarkable for the fact that she is in her sixties. She is wearing
glasses, looking intently at the portrait. Hers is the face of an
artist; suffered, still suffering, still wondering what life is about,
still romantic, still aware of what is going on around her.
Suddenly from her point of view we see a young man. Since
we are looking through her glasses, as it were, he is blurry,
indistinct. We turn to the portrait, which we see quite clearly. We
pull back to see ADRIENNE *middle distance looking at the*
portrait. We see her, almost slyly, take her glasses off to get a
better look at the young man.

On the young man. He is WILLIAM O'HARA; *dark-haired, in his*
late twenties. He is holding a programme in his hand. When he
senses ADRIENNE's *response, he looks down at the programme,*
then up quickly again, catching her in the act. Their eyes hold, but
then ADRIENNE *moves quickly again.*

ADRIENNE MARK *is a distinguished writer. Born and brought*
up in France, she wrote, as a young woman, a novel which became
an international success. A film was made in France, from this
book, and this too was an international success. ADRIENNE
developed an intense sympathy for America and wrote books from
the point of view of an enthusiastic Democrat who had put Europe
behind her. Thus, we may say she is a little in the tradition of
Sanche de Grammont who changed his name to Ted Morgan. But
only a little. ADRIENNE *is French to the core, and this is coming*
to the surface as our story opens. She is forced to admit she doesn't
understand America any more. Her books about America no
longer sell, and she is broke. This breaking up of a well-formed

personality is what she is enduring now. Something else is pulling her and this something is her childhood in France.

WILLIAM *is a serious young man who, although American born and bred, is in something like the same dilemma. That is, he inhabits a classic American archetype, and since he has a manly and direct nature, he does it with full force, but more and more he feels like a fish out of water. His archetype is the Man Who Lives Adventurously. Since he is an original person he wouldn't put it this way but his goal is to be James Dean as an artist.*

THE TITLES.
ADRIENNE *and* WILLIAM's *movements have this rhythm.* ADRIENNE, *making it a point to follow her own instincts about what is interesting at the show, moves from object to object, with perfect serenity.* WILLIAM *follows her at a distance – let us say two or three objects away – but keeps his eye in synch with her movements. Now we see that* WILLIAM *has a small Sony camcorder with him. He tries to pick the right moment in his dance with* ADRIENNE *– and then raises his camera to his eyes and looks at* ADRIENNE's *head through the viewfinder and films. He gets away with it – or so he thinks. Actually,* ADRIENNE *sees what he is doing and chooses to ignore it. Now her composure loosens up a bit. Finally, she breaks rhythm, and to regain her serenity, looks up with directed interest at the work in front of her. It is another self-portrait of the artist naked. This does not help her, and* WILLIAM, *like a predator, sees his chance. All at once, as the titles end, he is at her side, like a trusted friend, reading to* ADRIENNE *from the catalogue.*

WILLIAM

'Dunnings' obsession with himself reached intense focus during the late '60s and early 1970s. At odds with a world in collapse, he shut himself up in a room made from objects discarded by others and observed his own body. "The landscape of a child of irony," he called it. He took particular pleasure in relating his study of his own nakedness to events in the outside world, especially the Vietnam War. Number 16, showing one half of his face, is entitled "General Westmoreland Toasting the Ghost of General MacArthur". Number 17, showing his forearm, is entitled "Diem Remembering Caesar".'

On three works by this artist showing a thin, wistful body with a long flaccid penis.

'Numbers 18, 19 and 20 are called "The Tet Offensive". Nowhere in the important oeuvre . . .'

ADRIENNE *interrupts him.*

ADRIENNE
I remember that young men used to say that the best places to pick up women were art galleries and libraries. In this disconcerting world I am glad there is some continuity [*looks up*] but there are my friends . . .

Indeed, ADRIENNE has spotted a knot of fashionable people who have also recognized her. Rather, ADRIENNE has spotted her agent WILLY KUNST, who, as usual, is surrounded. Ordinarily, ADRIENNE would merely say hello, but now, for reasons she doesn't quite understand, she embraces the protection offered by this group.

Meanwhile, a YOUNG WOMAN who is clearly interested in WILLIAM has come up to him full of 'we are all one' confidentiality.

YOUNG WOMAN
I saw you talking to Adrienne Mark.

WILLIAM (*not eager to continue this conversation*)
Yes, I know.

YOUNG WOMAN
Picked her up on instinct? That's great. [*Significantly*] Great instinct. I like great instinct.

WILLIAM
I didn't pick her up.

YOUNG WOMAN
It sure looked like you did. [*Looking at 'Tet Offensive'*] I love this stuff. [*Sees that* WILLIAM *is about to head off*] I don't mind rejection – or much of anything else either if I like the man. My last name is Freemder. I'm the only Freemder in the book.

This much WILLIAM *hears and acknowledges with a nod, but he is retreating from the* YOUNG WOMAN *across the room, so this last part of her speech is to herself as she stands alone in front of 'Tet Offensive'.*

YOUNG WOMAN (*continuing*)
F. Freemder. I use the initial to keep the freaks away.

2   EXT.   MUSEUM OF MODERN ART. DAY.
WILLIAM *arrives at the curb in time to see* ADRIENNE *and her friends, including* WILLY, *driving off in a taxi.*

3   INT.   WILLIAM O'HARA'S LOFT. NIGHT.
Later that night. A clock reads ten-thirty p.m. WILLIAM *is studying Media and Media Theory, but he is poor. That is, he also has a full time job. His apartment shows the two sides of his nature. His possessions, as they relate to his social life and his person, are simple, almost working class. Jeans. Leather jacket. He has a shelf of books by* ADRIENNE MARK *including* Call Me French *in both French and English. On the wall above his books is a poster for* Call Me French – *French version. The Director's name is in large type. It is 'Un Film de* FRANZ LEGENDRE'. *We pan this to show the line 'based on the international best-seller by* ADRIENNE MARK'. *The French version of* Call Me French *was a film of 1962 or 1963.* WILLIAM's *other books are Schopenhauer, Adorno, Nietzsche, anyone who had the answers. There is a third side of him – his interest in film. The only expensive items in the*

room are five monitors and two VCRs. *Now watching (via VCR) the French version of* Call Me French. *One of the first French 'New Wave' films. It was made from* ADRIENNE*'s first, and most successful novel; it was later remade in Hollywood. The remake was vulgar and is now forgotten, but it did begin* ADRIENNE*'s American career. It was a film of 1969 or 1970.*

WILLIAM *lies in boxer shorts on his bed, a remote in his hand.*

He clicks on a monitor with the remote. He has five monitors and two VCRs connected into a kind of poor man's media centre, that is, it isn't expensive stuff he has – just Sears Brand Central, but hooked up to aid his cultural thinking.

On the screen of the monitor he has clicked on. It is playing Call Me French *French version. We don't hear any dialogue;* WILLIAM *is using the mute.*

On a YOUNG GIRL (MARCELLE). *She is shivering, really scared. The shot is very contemporary – that is, it reminds us of a million photographs we have seen this month in fashion magazines.*

WILLIAM *freezes the frame. Then he clicks on another TV set (he has five piled one on top of each other). He surfs the TV. We see many commercial images – MTV, a* GIRL *slurping a peach into her mouth against an industrial setting etc. – which reminds us of the loneliness and anomie of many 'new wave' films. He gets up and puts a tape into VCR number two. He goes back to his bed.*

Now we are going to see a few frames of the Hollywood remake of Call Me French. *It is rather in the spirit of Warren Beatty's* Shampoo. *Overblown, obviously sexual, with an 'easy' ironic humour.*

We see TWO MEN *and a* GIRL *in a luxurious hotel suite (style of 1969). One* MAN *is dark, slicked hair, early thirties. His* BUDDY *(Kris Kristofferson type) is a few years older. The* GIRL *is coiffured, young starlet type.*

In addition to the scenes from the two movies, we also see the video footage of what WILLIAM *filmed at the* MOMA. *Using rudimentary editing equipment,* WILLIAM *is splicing images of* ADRIENNE *into the clips of* Call Me French. *What he says ('It changed everything', etc.) will be used for the voice-over of the film he is making. He can record it as such.*

WILLIAM, *using the remote (he has a little trouble with it), plays* VCR. WILLIAM *presses the 'mute' button, but the remote malfunctions. The screen flickers. He presses the remote too hard, and the VCR flickers and goes off.* WILLIAM *throws away the remote in disgust.*

WILLIAM

Fuck it.

As he scrambles around trying to find another remote, he tries to fix his thought in his mind.

WILLIAM (*looks up at poster*)

It changed everything. The way we look at women; the way we look at film. That moment of spontaneity . . .

The new remote works. He turns the remake viciously off and turns on VCR number one. Once again we are watching the original version of Call Me French.

WILLIAM

It changed everything. The way we look at women; the way we look at film. That moment of spontaneity . . . the vulnerability of flesh; the importance of flesh . . . She integrated fright into sexuality, which is, in our disintegrating world, what we all must be brave enough to dare to do.

Suddenly, of itself, the second VCR comes on. Once again we see the TWO MALE LEADS *of the remake. The* COIFFURED GIRL *is sitting alone on a couch. She looks first at the* DARK-HAIRED MAN (*sultry look*), *then at the Kris Kristofferson type ('what can a girl do?' look). Then the* TWO MEN *look meaningfully ('Oh boy!') at one another.*

WILLIAM
Hollywood remakes suck.

3A   EXT.   ADRIENNE'S UPPER WEST SIDE APARTMENT.
DAY.
WILLY *and* ADRIENNE *arrive in a taxi in front of her apartment*
building. ADRIENNE *gets out of the taxi.*

WILLY (*still in taxi*)
Shall I see you?

ADRIENNE *blows him a kiss and walks into her building.*

3B   INT.   ADRIENNE'S UPPER WEST SIDE APARTMENT.
DAY.
In the corridor in front of her apartment door. The telephone is
ringing as ADRIENNE *is trying to get the key out of her bag,*
frantically. She rushes into her apartment to the phone. When she
finally reaches it, it has stopped ringing. A few seconds later, it
starts again. It is ELLIOTT *calling from Paris.*

ADRIENNE
Elliott? Why are you calling at this ungodly hour?

ELLIOTT
I've been calling you for a while, but there was no
answer.

ADRIENNE
What is it?

ELLIOTT
Fan Fan has died.

ADRIENNE (*pause*)
Good riddance.

ELLIOTT
Yes . . . uhm . . . he left no will and had no relatives. He

died bankrupt. Raymond says the apartment will be auctioned off by the state in a few months.

4   INT.   BEDROOM OF ADRIENNE'S UPPER WEST SIDE APARTMENT. NIGHT.

The middle of the night. ADRIENNE is having a nightmare. Pan the room. It has a luxurious belle époque *atmosphere.*

Start with sound only, taking over from ambient room noise, i.e. traffic, ticking of clock, etc.

5   INT.   LIVING ROOM OF LARGE PRIVATE TOWN HOUSE. EVENING.

ADRIENNE's nightmare. An aristocratic birthday party of 1943. A big birthday cake with eleven candles. The party consists of SIX YOUNG GIRLS *in costume and* JUDITH MARKOWSKY ('MADELEINE'), *Adrienne's mother, in the centre of what amounts to a* tableau vivant. JUDITH *turns to left and right.* JUDITH *does not look up – she does not notice* ADRIENNE *or try to say anything to her. Rather she is concerned only with the birthday party and the* SIX GIRLS *there. One* YOUNG GIRL *steps forward. Show* ADRIENNE *in her bed, very restless now. Back to the* YOUNG GIRL.

YOUNG GIRL
You really ought to have stayed at her side.

If you wanted to you could have saved her . . .

She looks at – or points to – a man off to the side. He is seated at a table of his own, dressed like a dandy, eating a slice of birthday cake. He is FAN FAN.

Note: The cake in front of the GIRLS *with the candles in it is whole and unsliced.* FAN FAN's *slice of cake is identical but does not come from theirs.*

The tableau of the birthday party superimposed on ADRIENNE *asleep. And then, just the tableau. We hold for a while and we notice something about it. It is very beautiful, but also quite eccentric. What seemed at first glance to be 'aristocratic' now shows itself to be, on second glance, Bohemian in an extreme way. The clothes the children are wearing, and, especially JUDITH's costumes are avant-garde, even Dada-esque. The juxtaposition of the fanciful artistic dress with the seriousness of the line 'she was saying that if you had wanted to you could have saved her', should be striking.*

5A INT.   ADRIENNE'S UPPER WEST SIDE APARTMENT. NIGHT.
ADRIENNE *wakes from her nightmare.*

Fade to black on which following words appear: SOME WEEKS LATER.

6 INT.   ADRIENNE'S APARTMENT. DAY.
ADRIENNE *has lived in this large, spacious West Side apartment for thirty years. The apartment reflects her taste, her character, and her turbulent past. Her taste is good. The objects she has chosen show a proud, informed, modern personality. Everything is strong – there is nothing merely decorative here. At the same time, there is a touch of confusion – almost of insecurity.*

Many of ADRIENNE's strong impulses are in conflict. She loves Edwardian luxury – but also modern defiance. Moreover, the objects here reflect a life which has taken many twists and turns over the three decades. We will want to show this, emphasizing in particular three epochs:

1) Early 1960s – the epoch of Call Me French *– novel and first film.*

2) Late 1960s – a period in which ADRIENNE *became involved in the youth culture of that time.*

3) The 1970s and later. Here we will want to show the other books she has written, the honours she has received and so forth.

Hollywood has figured in this period, and we may notice, for instance, a photograph of the 1970s remake of Call Me French. *She has been honoured by the American Academy – Institute of Arts and Letters; she has served on the Selection Committee of the John Guggenheim Foundation; she has been honoured by the Mayor of New York. Still, we understand, it is her early work which she enjoys the most.*

On her bookshelves there are many editions of Call Me French *in many translations – even Japanese. Her later books are in single copies. Their titles include* The War That is Pulling Us Apart, The Fire in Nebraska *and* Whitman's Ghost.

The camera soaks in the atmosphere of the apartment while we hear in the background Barbara Hendricks' version of 'Le nuit d'été' by Berlioz.

In the kitchen MILLY, *Adrienne's housekeeper, is putting a silver coffee pot on a tray. Everything about the tray is luxurious. The apartment may be West Side, but this breakfast tray looks like the Rothschilds and nothing but.*

We follow MILLY *with the tray through the dining room, which also has a formal air, into* ADRIENNE MARK's *bedroom. Adrienne's breakfast, by the way, consists of one soft boiled egg, coffee and three newspapers,* Le Monde, The New York Times *and the* New York Post.

ADRIENNE *has just awakened. Sleepy, a little out of sorts.*

MILLY
Good morning.

The tray is placed on Adrienne's bed. MILLY *stands a little disapproving.* ADRIENNE *rouses herself, sits up.* ADRIENNE *takes a linen napkin off the tray and unfolds it. Step one in the ritual is a glance at the papers – the* Post *first.*

ADRIENNE
What have we here? 'Killer Screams For Mercy'. No. 'Bronx Love Story.'

MILLY

Kennedys down the drain on page six. Currency traders rule the world business section.

ADRIENNE

You think the world's gone to hell.

MILLY

Don't you?

ADRIENNE

I think you're mad at me.

MILLY

You've been saying for thirty years the world is going to hell. No taste in Hollywood. Either it's no good or they don't make it like they used to.

ADRIENNE

And for thirty years you have been walking past disaster with perfect composure. I think you're mad at me. Come on, Milly, you're mad as you've ever been. It makes me very uncomfortable.

The telephone rings. MILLY *picks it up.*

MILLY

Mark residence. Who shall I say is calling?

Silence. MILLY *listens, then smiles, hands phone to* ADRIENNE. ADRIENNE *makes 'Who is it?' face.*

MILLY (*very matter-of-fact, but with raised eyebrow*)

Some young man who is afraid you might have the impression he tried to pick you up at the Museum. He sounds nice.

ADRIENNE

Milly!

But MILLY *has walked away leaving her with the phone in her hand, and* ADRIENNE *has said 'Hello' before she realizes it.*

91

ADRIENNE

No, you didn't give offence, Mr O'Hara. That's very sweet of you to say. No, I promise you I'm not offended. By the way, how did you happen to get this number? Well, that's right, it is in the book, but how did you know who I was? Oh, I see. [*Looks at* MILLY] I'm one of the most famous women in the world.

ADRIENNE *grimaces and mouths the words 'A fan' at* MILLY.

ADRIENNE (*now very dignified and remote*)

Well, I'm delighted, always, to find an enthusiastic reader. Oh you're in the phone book too. O'Hara. I'll be sure to remember. O'Hara, such a nice Irish name. [*More looking at* MILLY) There are other O'Haras in the book. And your name is William, and you live in Gansevoort Street. It's all completely understood: William O'Hara from Gansevoort Street, but now I must get about my busy day which will be eaten up with futilities to do with my imminent removal to France. Good bye, Mr O'Hara.

She hangs up the phone.

MILLY

So why weren't you nice to the young man? Could cheer you up. William O'Hara from Gansevoort Street. I'll remember.

The sound of the front doorbell is heard. MILLY *lets* BANCROFT *into the apartment.* BANCROFT *says, 'Oh, Adrienne.' It is a high-pitched cultivated voice, seductive and a little over-friendly, as he goes into* ADRIENNE's *bedroom, and* MILLY *follows.*

Apparently, BANCROFT *and* ADRIENNE *are on very friendly terms because he sits on* ADRIENNE's *bed.* MILLY *scowls at him and holds the silver coffee pot in front of her. Close-up on* MILLY's *hand – rubbing the pot furiously.*

ADRIENNE

Will you take coffee? Milly is just going to brew a fresh pot.

MILLY *holds the coffee pot in front of her, holding on for dear life, as it were.* BANCROFT *looks at the pot.*

BANCROFT

What a glorious coffee pot. I didn't notice it before.

BANCROFT's *character is such that when he sees a thing he likes, the human figures in the foreground seem to vanish. We see the room from his point of view now. The silver pot and nothing but. Next we hear* BANCROFT's *mental Christie's catalogue 'Fine Silver'; then the pages of the catalogue flip with incredible rapidity still in* BANCROFT's *mind – we hear a jubilant crowded group of* BUYERS *at an auction vying with one another to – but now he returns to himself; someone is talking to him.*

ADRIENNE

Harry – Mr Bancroft.

BANCROFT (*still a little abstracted. His
mind is still half in the imaginary sale*)

Sorry. You have some very fine things.

Now he refocuses: his charm is back on line for ADRIENNE.

ADRIENNE (*a little vulnerable to his charm*)

It wasn't a matter of effort . . .

BANCROFT (*lowering his voice to increase
charm*)

Of course not.

ADRIENNE

Or even of collecting . . .

BANCROFT's *attention half drifts to the coffee pot which* MILLY *is still rubbing furiously.*

BANCROFT

When one has an instinct.

MILLY *looks at* ADRIENNE. ADRIENNE, *a little reluctantly, looks at* MILLY. ADRIENNE *then does notice that* BANCROFT's *focus has once again drifted to the pot. She coughs. He looks up,* ADRIENNE's *look has changed. She is not vulnerable to his charm now.*

BANCROFT (*down a tone; now the consummate professional*)

I'm afraid you caught me zeroing in on that lovely, *lovely* pot.

ADRIENNE

You can't have it.

BANCROFT (*relaxes into a seductive mode*)

You know I know everything about silver. That's how I began, I camped out with Judge Untermeyer while he was forming his famous collection. You know the Untermeyer collection? Lamerie, practically all Lamerie.

MILLY

He get to keep it?

BANCROFT

What, Milly?

MILLY

Or did you take it away from him?

BANCROFT (*getting the point*)

Well, naturally, Milly, when he passed to his reward – at the time of his death. Yes, we handled the sale.

MILLY

Well, Miss Adrienne didn't pass to no reward yet.

ADRIENNE

Milly!

94

BANCROFT

It's cold out this morning.

ADRIENNE

It will be warmer in the living room, Harry, where I have laid out the wretched remnants of my material life.

BANCROFT (*now acting like a loyal employee, fairly jumps up and heads to the door*)
[*Like a suitor*] I'll be waiting!

ADRIENNE (*to* MILLY)

So why don't you like Mr Bancroft? You have my full attention.

MILLY

Seems like any time a man talks a certain way you back down – or blow up.

This has a ring of truth for ADRIENNE. *She looks at* MILLY *as though to say 'please go on'.*

MILLY (*continuing*)

And he snoops.

ADRIENNE

He's paid to snoop. Snooping is what these people do for a living. This is a large apartment. I've lived here for longer than I care to remember, I have things piled upon things, I'm not sure what's valuable and what isn't. I don't like your tone.

MILLY

That's where you used to take a drag on a Chesterfield, put it out and light another one.

ADRIENNE (*fierce*)

Of course he has the manner of someone who is looking for something. Because he *is* looking for something, anything. My possessions are . . .

95

MILLY

In the little drawer in the bookcase when he's supposed to be looking at the books and pictures.

ADRIENNE

This coffee is cold.

MILLY

I've had three husbands. The first one stole my money; the second one stole my clothes.

ADRIENNE *suddenly changes manner entirely. She lightens up. This is a woman who knows how to laugh.*

MILLY (*completely at one with* ADRIENNE
now)

Second one was Roderick. He'd be goin' through the laundry basket. I'd say, 'He's the domestic type is all.' Then one day I come home and he dressed like me head to toe, lip-synching my songs. That's why, when I decided to marry my husband Frank, I let him move in with me first. Worked out fine. Fifteen years and he doesn't know where the dirty laundry is . . .

ADRIENNE

Anyway I *am* sure there's nothing wrong with Harry Bancroft. He's just not your type, that's all.

7 INT.   EDWARDIAN ROOM, PLAZA HOTEL. DAY.
ADRIENNE *with* WILLY KUNST, *her agent.*

ADRIENNE

I'm not sure I'm ready to go back to Paris . . .

WILLY

It's not a question of ready. You have to. That's all there is to it.

ADRIENNE

You can't stay in New York for thirty years and not become a New Yorker.

96

WILLY

Oh yes you can. Look at me. To be or not to be. That is the issue. I can't wait to get your next book. Frankly, as to New York, you're played out. You don't like it here any more and you don't write any more. Your audience is dwindling – you need to recharge.

ADRIENNE (*with angry sarcasm*)

Thank you very much. You're the kindest man in the world.

WILLY (*triumphant*)

Willy Kunst is nobody's fool, plus he's a good friend, plus he has a natural language gift.

ADRIENNE (*suddenly serious*)

Willy . . . Every month – at least ten or twelve times a year – I have the same dream. It is my eleventh birthday. My mother is trying to tell me something. She tries and tries but I can never hear what she is saying. Last night it came again – but with a difference. One of the little girls at the party stepped forward and said something.

WILLY

What?

ADRIENNE

She said that if I tried I could have saved my mother. [*Pause*] I remember the day quite clearly. It must have been 1943. Just think, the Germans were occupying Paris, and we . . . [*Looks directly at* WILLY] dressed up and *played* at having a birthday party.

WILLY

A party is a party.

ADRIENNE (*a small laugh*)

Our parties weren't just parties. My mother was insistently avante-garde. She lived partly in the past, and partly in the future. And Fan Fan.

WILLY

The guy who just died? Whose apartment you want to buy back?

ADRIENNE

It was not his apartment. My mother put it in his name so as to have no hassles with the Germans. He was supposed to give it back to us once things blew over. Things didn't blow over and he ended up with the apartment. Convenient, *n'est-ce pas?* I'm sure he denounced her. Needless to say, I never saw him again. Never saw the apartment either.

WILLY

My Adrienne is finally opening up. I'm flabbergasted. What was Fan Fan like?

ADRIENNE

He was a dandy. A dandy from an illustrious line of . . . greengrocers! My mother liked that. She wouldn't have liked a real gentleman.

WILLY

Now listen to me. Pretend I'm a gypsy. I interpret your dream. Go to Paris like a civilized person and write about . . . things.

ADRIENNE

Like how I was strangely rescued. My mother, one day, packed all my prettiest clothes, and took me to the house of my best friend. Her parents were bankers, rich as anything. They liked me. My mother spent the day with us. I mean my mother and I spent the day with this family. I was to be there for a weekend visit. There were many, too many clothes for a weekend visit. I ended up staying many, many years.

WILLY (*emphatically telling* ADRIENNE)

That's good. Write about that. Plus other things. Secret things that the rest of us don't know because we're not as smart as you are.

This is a deep rare compliment WILLY *is paying to* ADRIENNE *and she appreciates it.*

WILLY

Plus you've suffered but you can still smile.

WILLY *is suddenly adamant. Raises his voice as if talking to a child.*

WILLY

There are millions of people waiting to hear such a thing. You could have another hit!

A moment's silence. This rings a bell with ADRIENNE.

WILLY

Even me. I don't understand my own life. I am born in Vienna. When I am little – three years old – my nurse, bless her forever, she was a sweetheart, I supported her for thirty years, year in year out, no regard for myself, lean cows or cows for the slaughter it makes no difference, I mail her a cheque – my nurse takes me out on the Ringstrasse and – there is the Emperor, Kaiser Franz Josef – bless him too, I guess, he was a hell of an Emperor – as Emperors go you understand; I don't know too much from an Emperor, but . . .

ADRIENNE

Please, Willy. Cut to the chase.

WILLY

Why are the Habsburgs on television? I cut to the chase. I leave Vienna. The Emperors go away, I am a little boy in steerage. I come to America. Everything is new. Everything is the future. Now the future is shopping channel. OK. Everybody shops. So I have dinner with Myra Frannel, nice woman, her father was a big man in Boston, the kind wouldn't even speak to a Jew, and I say good night, and watch a little TV. Everything is just what I already know except Christian Television, which I don't want, and Chinese soap operas which I don't need and shopping channel. So I shop a while, and there she is. So-and-so Princess Von Habsburg selling the Habsburg Crown Jewels? So what is that? What happened to them?

WAITER *approaches, deferential.*

WAITER
Is everything satisfactory, Mr Kunst?

WILLY
Very satisfactory, thank you. [*To* ADRIENNE] Go to Paris. Buy your mother's house. Tell secrets.

8   OMITTED IN FINAL VERSION.

9   EXT.   A SMALL DRESS SHOP. DAY.
ADRIENNE, *deep in thought, almost bumps into* TWO LADIES *as they leave the shop. One of the ladies says a word or two in French.* ADRIENNE's *attention is drawn to the shop. Intercut* ADRIENNE *looking into the window, there are dresses in the windows on mannequins – various sizes – to window of 'Madeleine', the Dress-making establishment of Adrienne's mother,* JUDITH.

10   INT.   'MADELEINE' – PARIS. FLASHBACK. DAY.
1943. The establishment of Adrienne's mother JUDITH – called 'Madeleine'. This is a fashionable establishment – a dressmaker's establishment rather than haute couture, but high style.

Our model might be 'Alix' – the establishment run by Madame Gres before the war. Two dresses are being brought into the front of the shop, with considerable fanfare by YOUNG ADRIENNE *(a girl of eleven, say) and one of her mother's assistants. An* ARISTOCRATIC FRENCH LADY *is seated, watching this presentation. The two dresses are put on* TWO MANNE-QUINS. FLASHBACK TO: TWO LIVE MANNEQUINS. ADRIENNE *stands to one side;* JUDITH *is describing the two* dresses to the ARISTOCRATIC LADY, who is taking great pleasure in the process. First she asks to have one mannequin turned around so she can have a closer look, then the other. She appears to have a friendly, if distant, attitude towards ADRIENNE. Finally, grand style, she rises, orders one dress. On this we see again the name 'Madeleine'.

CLOSE ON: a smile between ADRIENNE and JUDITH. This has been a big sale. JUDITH'S ASSISTANT takes the dress ordered by the lady off the mannequin and into the back of the shop, leaving. ADRIENNE rushes and gives JUDITH a hug. We see the dress over her shoulder.

CUT TO: The dress shop in modern times on Fifth Avenue. We see ADRIENNE's reflection in the plate glass window.

11   EXT.   CENTRAL PARK. DAY.
ADRIENNE walks on through Central Park. The Mall. Ahead of her is an attractive AFRICAN-AMERICAN WOMAN of nineteen or twenty years old. A young career woman. Around her neck is a simple gold chain. All at once, a GANG OF FOUR YOUTHS, ages 14–16, rush her. All this is very quick. ONE BOY distracts the YOUNG WOMAN, the OTHER grabs her gold necklace, and they run.

ADRIENNE goes to help her, but the woman turns away as if she doesn't need her help. This is why she is leaving New York – not just the violence, but the fact that she feels she has no solution for it, that there is no way for her to help.

ADRIENNE is walking north. Sees family having a picnic with plenty of food. Smart young picnickers pop a champagne bottle which triggers flashback at Maxim's.

12   INT.   FLASHBACK. MAXIM'S. 1943. NIGHT.
Maitre d' is ordering people about. A waiter is opening a bottle of champagne. A table laid as for a banquet. ADRIENNE has run ahead of JUDITH, her mother's lover FAN FAN and a LAWYER

to look at this splendid table. *Now we have a closer look at* ADRIENNE *herself. What we notice are her eyes which are big and have a deep look. They are not quite a child's eyes. And they love to take everything in. She looks at the table. We see* JUDITH, FAN FAN *and the* LAWYER *move towards the table.* ADRIENNE, *as these others are seating themselves, looks around the restaurant. She is in a reverie, but we notice some disturbing things. A group of* GERMAN OFFICERS. *A newspaper with a reference to German 'Victories'.*

CUT TO: *A few minutes later. Everyone is seated.* FAN FAN *is talking. The* LAWYER *has a small leather envelope.* JUDITH *seems hesitant, anxious but eager not to appear this way.* FAN FAN *has a big 'I can handle anything' air.*

> ### ADRIENNE
> Oh, Mother, these petits fours are exquisite. Don't you agree, Fan Fan?

Picking one up and eating it, FAN FAN *replies.*

> ### FAN FAN
> Exquisite, my princess, exquisite.

ADRIENNE, *playing make-believe, lets an imaginary gentleman kiss her hand. She may even curtsey.*

ARISTOCRATIC LADY, *wearing the dress she has brought from 'Madeleine', and a* GRAND GENTLEMAN *enter the restaurant.*

Now from ADRIENNE's *point of view we see the* ARISTOCRATIC LADY *from 'Madeleine' sitting with a* GRAND GENTLEMAN. *She is wearing the dress we saw her take from Adrienne's mother's shop. We see instantaneously that the* ARISTOCRATIC LADY *is in a very different mood now from the slightly generous one she was in while choosing a dress at 'Madeleine'. This man she is with is* grande chose. *She is leaning forward towards him — doing her best to impress.*

> ### FAN FAN (to LAWYER and JUDITH)
> Shall we finish our unpleasant business before we eat?

LAWYER

Of course.

ADRIENNE (*pulled out of her reverie*)
What unpleasant business?

JUDITH

Yes, Adrienne is right. What unpleasant business? These papers are a mere formality. A tiny precaution.

She takes the documents and signs 'Judith Mark'.

JUDITH

Voilà. Now they will look and see that my house is owned by François-Pierre de Castéllane. [*Picking up her champagne glass*] To Fan Fan.

The LAWYER *looks down at papers.*

LAWYER

I'm sorry. Could you sign your real name.

The LAWYER *senses* ADRIENNE *looking at him. He knows, if* ADRIENNE *doesn't, that this selling of the house has a baleful side. He looks up almost apologetically at* ADRIENNE. ADRIENNE *frowns.*

JUDITH

My real name?

LAWYER

Yes, Markowsky . . . if I am not mistaken.

ADRIENNE'S MOTHER *winces, as if slapped in the face.*

During this exchange, ADRIENNE *rises, quite like a grand lady herself and as though she did it all the time, walks to the* ARISTOCRATIC LADY. *The moment she gets up* HER MOTHER *stops dead in her tracks.* FAN FAN *too. The* LAWYER *more baleful than ever. A kind of dead silence in the restaurant. Everyone but* ADRIENNE *knows that this world of fantasy and pleasure is shot through with corruption and terror.*

103

All of a sudden, ADRIENNE'S MOTHER *realizes that* ADRIENNE *is on her way to the* ARISTOCRATIC LADY's *table.*

ADRIENNE (*lost in her own reverie*)
Madam La Comtesse! May I say how well you are dressed!

This is meant to be friendly, naive and worldly at the same time. The ARISTOCRATIC LADY *is horrified.*

ADRIENNE
I think clothes cut on the bias fall so nicely. Don't you agree?

LADY
I really think you must have mistaken me for someone else.

MAN
Ah – your dressmaker.

LADY
Oh yes . . . possibly.

MAN
You know them socially?

LADY
Of course not.

MAN
Jewish?

As he says this, we see two officers greeting each other with a Nazi salute in background.

LADY
Of course not.

MAN (*vicious*)
And my dear, I thought you *more* a woman of the world.

ADRIENNE *has stood frozen during this. Just as though she had* been rendered immobile by a blast of icy wind. We see her now from JUDITH's point of view. Slowly, with infinite bravery, JUDITH rises from the table where she has felt some protection and walks across the minefield this situation is for her to ADRIENNE's side.

> JUDITH (*to* ADRIENNE)
> Take my hand.

ADRIENNE *and* JUDITH *walk back to the table, where FAN FAN has risen, smiling.* ADRIENNE *is zombie-like now, and merely sits without comment.* JUDITH *seems about to sit herself, but something comes to her – a bit of old ferocious energy, and she returns to the* ARISTOCRATIC LADY.

> JUDITH
> Countess. You are wearing my dress. A dress you have not paid for, and do not wear with any understanding. [*Defiantly*] Eight thousand francs, Countess. You owe me for that dress. [*Ferocious*] The child liked you. I spit in your eye.

From ADRIENNE's point of view – watching her mother.

CUT TO: The FASHIONABLE COUPLE's table:

JUDITH turns without waiting for an answer. The Countess stares straight ahead.

ADRIENNE's point of view: JUDITH walking with grim deliberation back to her table. Adrienne's mother has done something which has transformed, for a moment, the atmosphere of the restaurant. The FASHIONABLE COUPLE have been defeated. The WAITERS look on her with respect. Even the GERMAN OFFICERS seem to be impressed by her great bravery. FAN FAN alone is jittery.

> FAN FAN
> You should not have done that.

JUDITH
Nonetheless, I did it.

CLOSE-UP *on* YOUNG ADRIENNE's *face: infinite love and admiration for her mother, even though she is still unaware of exactly what has happened.*

13   EXT.   CENTRAL PARK. DAY.
ADRIENNE *in Central Park. She leaves the mall and cuts across the grass towards Central Park West.*

Her determination breaks down. Her stride breaks.

She is alone in a lonely landscape. She pulls herself together and walks to Central Park West.

14   EXT.   ADRIENNE'S APARTMENT. DAY.
As ADRIENNE *approaches her building she sees her doorman hail a cab. On second glance he now seems to be dressed in the uniform of one of the German officers from the scene at Maxim's. We see the taxi pull up to a stop. She is now closer to the doorman and sees the familiar face she knows. He smiles and offers a friendly greeting as she passes him in silence.*

15   INT.   ELEVATOR – ADRIENNE'S APARTMENT. DAY.
In the elevator. The ELEVATOR MAN *observes a strange and disturbed* ADRIENNE. *She is upset. She is suddenly in a rage.*

She composes herself; arrives at her floor and gets out.

16   INT.   ADRIENNE'S APARTMENT. DAY.
ADRIENNE *fumbles through her purse for her keys, and cannot find them. She rings the bell mercilessly, torturing herself. Then she thumps the door – almost in a fit of madness.*

ADRIENNE (*her voice is deep, furious*)
I can't get into my own house. I can't get into my own house.

The door is opened by MILLY.

MILLY
What's wrong?

ADRIENNE *holds out her purse helplessly.* MILLY *takes her purse, looks inside and pulls out the keys.*

17   INT.   ADRIENNE'S APARTMENT. DAY.
The apartment a few hours later. In ADRIENNE's *study,* ADRIENNE *and* BANCROFT. ADRIENNE *has spread out dozens of possessions for him to look at. Paintings, a Lion d'Or award from Venice. She is just opening a cabinet when* MILLY *comes in.*

MILLY
That boy called again.

ADRIENNE
Get rid of him.

MILLY
He just wants to meet you. Give him a break. I told him you'd call back.

MILLY, *significantly, puts a piece of paper on* ADRIENNE's *desk.*

ADRIENNE
Milly!

MILLY
He just wants to help. Give him a break.

BANCROFT *has been looking at a portrait of young Adrienne. It is quite obvious that this portrait is a hit. We see the room from his point of view now. The portrait of young Adrienne and nothing but. The next sequence is incredibly fast. We see (*BANCROFT's

107

mental picture) a Christie's catalogue 'The Adrienne Mark Collection'; then the pages of the catalogue flip with incredible rapidity to a photograph of the portrait in the catalogue; then for one split second – still in BANCROFT's mind – we hear a jubilant crowded group of BUYERS AT AN AUCTION vying with one another to bid on the portrait.

The study a little later. The contents of the cabinet have now been spread out. They relate to the French version of the film made from Adrienne's book Call Me French. ADRIENNE and BANCROFT sit at the table. ADRIENNE is under BANCROFT's spell and does not relate to MILLY, who looks very serious and disapproving. BANCROFT ignores MILLY entirely. ADRIENNE pours him a cup of coffee.

18   EXT.   THE MEAT-PACKING DISTRICT. DAY.
WILLIAM O'HARA's loft on Gansevoort Street. WILLIAM is watching a scene from the French version of Call Me French.

19   OMITTED IN FINAL VERSION.

20   INT.   A DRESS SHOP. PARIS. DAY.
CALL ME FRENCH ORIGINAL. BLACK AND WHITE.

NADINE, a dark-haired woman of thirty with a customer. NADINE is brusque, powerful, from the lower middle class. THEODORE enters. NADINE immediately brushes off the customer she is with, pulls down the shade on the door of the shop. Immediately THEODORE just takes her; hikes up her skirt, puts her up on a counter and fucks her. It's quite short, but intense. And, apparently, a matter of custom. After the act is completed, NADINE arranges herself quite quickly and pulls up the shade.

THEODORE
I'll need you in five minutes.

21   OMITTED IN FINAL VERSION.

22 INT.   LOFT OVER SHOP. DAY.
CALL ME FRENCH ORIGINAL. BLACK AND WHITE

Next, we see THEODORE *opening a door. We are in a loft space over the shop. There are boxes of thread and so forth around in this space with an industrial feel. Within is a young well-born girl named* FRANCE, *about sixteen. Very good looking, with intelligent eyes. There is a scar on her cheek.*

FRANCE

I was waiting for you.

THEODORE

Evidemment. Shall we begin?

He lights a spotlight, directing it towards her eyes, as if for an interrogation.

THEODORE

Name?

FRANCE

France.

THEODORE

Nationality?

FRANCE

Française . . . [*Smiles*] *évidemment.*

THEODORE (*screams*)

Stick to the facts! Nationality?

FRANCE (*poutingly*)

Française.

THEODORE

What is chapter one in the story of your life?

FRANCE

I don't know . . . My birth, I guess.

THEODORE

Shut up! You can't know. [*To* NADINE, *who is in a corner, scornfully*] Her birth, she says.

FRANCE

If I can't know, who can?

THEODORE

Come here, Nadine.

NADINE *enters the frame.*

THEODORE

What is chapter one in the story of her life?

NADINE (*flatly, as if reading*)

Theo walked up to her and spread apart her thighs.

THEODORE *goes towards her and spreads her thighs.*

DISSOLVE TO:

NADINE

Chapter two. Nadine approached her slowly. France turned her scarred cheek towards her. She licked her scar.

DISSOLVE TO: FRANCE, *scar in profile; she turns and looks directly into the camera.*

FRANCE VOICE-OVER

Je m'appelle France.

23 INT. WILLIAM O'HARA'S LOFT. DAY.

FREEZE FRAME. *Pull back to see* WILLIAM, *who is in boxer shorts, lying on his bed with a remote in his hand. He rewinds for a few seconds, mutes the sound and finds the shot of* FRANCE. *He slo-mo's it down to the last shot (above).*

WILLIAM (*deep contentment, lying back in relaxed fashion on his bed*)

It was great, so great.

24 INT. ADRIENNE'S APARTMENT. DAY.

*The next afternoon ADRIENNE and HARRY BANCROFT.
Now in ADRIENNE's study. She is not happy. BANCROFT is
getting on her nerves; plus she is sick of all this buying and selling.
Now, she is the client; allowing BANCROFT no personal liber-
ties. The door from the study to the hall is open and MILLY passes
by, seemingly in a casual way; in fact she is keeping a close eye on
ADRIENNE.*

> ADRIENNE
>
> In here we have drawings: Cocteau, Dali, Giacometti,
> Bernard Buffet . . . And a few objects, too . . . This plate
> by Picasso. A dear friend. Such a bad boy. I have always
> liked bad boys when they had genius. Did you know him?

> BANCROFT
>
> Picasso?

> ADRIENNE
>
> Yes; that's who we were talking of. Picasso.

> BANCROFT
>
> No, I didn't know him.

> ADRIENNE
>
> Your work has brought you into contact with collectors
> then, more than artists?

> BANCROFT
>
> I suppose that would have been inevitable. Yes . . . If you
> are tired, or unwell.

> ADRIENNE
>
> Not at all.

*Once more, MILLY has passed by the open door. This time she
has looked enquiringly at ADRIENNE who has not acknowledged
the look.*

> ADRIENNE
>
> Let's keep going.

BANCROFT *picks up a small portrait.*

                    BANCROFT
This woman is . . .

                    ADRIENNE
Well it's me, everywhere. [*Gesturing to all the pictures*] Is
that a problem? . . . I mean, would that make it harder to
sell?

                    BANCROFT
Not at all. No, in fact . . .

The phone rings.

                    ADRIENNE
Would you excuse me for a moment?

                    BANCROFT
Please . . .

ADRIENNE *goes next door to answer the phone. As soon as she's
speaking on the phone,* BANCROFT *goes over to the portrait of
Adrienne as a child.*

                ADRIENNE (*on phone*)
Willy, darling . . . Yes . . . NO! Don't bring them now
please. One more buyer. One more buyer and I will go
mad . . . NOT NOW . . . [*Pause – WILLY is insisting*] . . .
YES YES YES YOU APPALLING MAN . . . YES.

When ADRIENNE *returns to* BANCROFT *they are in very different
moods.* ADRIENNE *is in a suppressed rage.* BANCROFT *is in a
greedy reverie thanks to the portrait. He holds the picture in front of
him – just as if it were on the block right now.*

                    BANCROFT
This one is very nice.

                    ADRIENNE
Harry, I'm afraid I'm very tired and we'll have to call it a
day.

25 INT. ADRIENNE'S APARTMENT. DAY.

Later, ADRIENNE is in the kitchen, helping MILLY go through cabinets and refrigerator and looking through her freezer.

ADRIENNE
I insist that you take this food home, Milly.

The doorbell rings.

ADRIENNE
Willy Kunst is bringing more treasure hunters. I dread it.

25A INT. ADRIENNE'S APARTMENT. DAY.

WILLY KUNST enters. A rich YOUNG TEXAN COUPLE. The YOUNG TEXANS are about thirty, very attractive and in a way sympathetic. They don't mind about their money – or people's attitude towards it – at all. They just want to have fun. Juxtapose ADRIENNE at her wit's end; MILLY standing behind her; WILLY exuberant – and these incredibly healthy carefree rich people.

25B INT. ADRIENNE'S APARTMENT. DAY.

A few minutes later. ADRIENNE has made a feeble attempt to be hospitable. Cocktails, perhaps. MILLY looking over her worriedly. The MAN is stretched out in a chair – doesn't really care where he is – the world belongs to him.

WOMAN
I decided not to be a timid soul. Isn't that right, honey? I said to myself, just do it. Like Grant took Richmond. Isn't that right, honey?

MAN
Just like Grant took Richmond.

WOMAN
I got it. Jack Kerouac's cap. The one he wore. Can you believe it?

She really expects to get a response from this. ADRIENNE has a kind of grim smile. WILLY and MILLY involuntarily exchange a glance.

> WOMAN (*wanting to make it crystal clear*)
> At auction. I got Jack Kerouac's cap. Johnny Depp got the raincoat.

WOMAN takes out cap from an envelope and passes it around.

ADRIENNE's eyes open wide in pure horror.

At this, ADRIENNE flees. As simple as that – as though her sanity depended on it. She seems terribly young as she goes. In this spirit she left Paris thirty years ago, perhaps. It got to be too much and she just packed up and left. The TEXANS look after her. WILLY, in a frenetic tone, fills the gap with his volume.

> WILLY
> Incredible woman. Artistic temperament!

MILLY stands by disapproving. Almost a surrogate for ADRIENNE. WILLY's tone remains at high volume.

> WILLY
> Always I have given you good advice. The best! And now I say live where a great writer lived. Buy the apartment.

> WOMAN
> Oh, Willy, we want it *all*!

> MAN
> Look, dear.

This moment ADRIENNE walks in. She looks, again with horror, at the scene in her marvellous house, the place where she has lived and worked for thirty years. It is already a yard sale. First she looks with fury at WILLY. But then her eyes are riveted on the portrait being held by the MAN. We see the portrait from her point of view as the WOMAN makes one last attempt to converse with her.

ADRIENNE *looking at the portrait.*

> ### WOMAN
> Mamma just loved silver and paintings. She specialized.
> Did you ever hear about Lamerie, Mrs Mark?

> ### ADRIENNE (*zombie-like, turning to the*
> ### WOMAN)
> Well, yes as a matter of fact.

> ### WOMAN
> Well, Mama specialized in him and now I want to
> specialize in . . . *you!*

WILLY *takes one look at* ADRIENNE'*s expression and takes
immediate action. This is Grant taking Richmond. He simply
bundles the* TEXANS *towards the door.*

> ### WILLY
> All over! Must go! Russian Tea Room. We must! They
> give away tables. Out, out, brief candle!

The TEXANS *allow themselves to be bundled and their feelings
are not hurt in the least.* WILLY *returns to loudly whisper one
thing to* ADRIENNE.

> ### WILLY
> Willy Kunst will handle all! Like Grant took. What did
> Grant take, Milly?

26 INT.   ADRIENNE'S STUDY IN THE APARTMENT.
DAY.
ADRIENNE *has a slip of paper in her hand. 'William O'Hara' it
says. She punches in the number.*

> ### ADRIENNE
> Mr O'Hara? What about right now.

27 INT.   A FASHIONABLE RESTAURANT IN THE

MEAT-PACKING DISTRICT. DAY.
WILLIAM *is in the kitchen with his friend* BOBBY *and* EMILIO,
*the owner of the restaurant. Through the door we see the
restaurant proper, which is by no means full.* WILLIAM, *almost
involuntarily, helping* BOBBY *with preparations.*

WILLIAM
Get this. She blew smoke into James Dean's face. I swear.
Just before he died. She's one of the most famous women
in the world.

EMILIO
OK. OK. You work Friday, Saturday. Order what you
want. And no bill.

BOBBY
And a good table.

EMILIO (*wistfully looking at half-empty restaurant*)
And a good table.

28   INT.   THE RESTAURANT. DAY.
BOBBY *and* WILLIAM.

WILLIAM
Stay close, but don't hover.

BOBBY
I know how to wait on celebrities.

WILLIAM
You know how to wait on models and rap stars. You
don't know how to wait on her.

BOBBY
You got a thing for older chicks, man?

WILLIAM
I got a thing for the real thing, man. Schopenhauer, not
Derrida. Know what I'm saying?

BOBBY

Don't know, don't care.

WILLIAM

So, stay close, but don't hover. [ADRIENNE *enters*]
There she is.

WILLIAM *goes to meet* ADRIENNE, *then turns for one over-the-shoulder word to* BOBBY.

WILLIAM

And don't recite the specials. Just bring the menu.

See ADRIENNE *and* WILLIAM *from* BOBBY's *point of view.*
WILLIAM, *gallant, almost makes a small bow, and escorts*
ADRIENNE *to the table. They are seated.* BOBBY *comes to*
the table immediately. Frankly, he is hovering.

BOBBY

Hello, I'm your waiter, Bobby.

WILLIAM *grimaces.*

BOBBY, *who is a nice guy, not sophisticated, becomes flustered.*

BOBBY

Our special today is . . .

WILLIAM *glares at him, maybe tugs at his apron.* BOBBY
recollects himself.

BOBBY

The menu!

Hands menu to ADRIENNE *and* WILLIAM.

An hour later. The restaurant. The lunch is working. BOBBY *is*
calm, impeccable. WILLIAM *is talking with great animation, and*
ADRIENNE *is listening with concentration.*

117

WILLIAM

The media is destroying itself in this country and taking the country with it. The media was the forum for ordinary citizens. Now, it takes what they had already – their dignity.

ADRIENNE *continues to eat.*

WILLIAM

And the intellectuals engage in masturbatory fantasies. The exhibition where we met – that was so real for us. This is what Mr Jackson of the *Times* said:

Just as WILLIAM *begins to read what Jackson of the* Times *wrote, he realizes that what he most wants to do is to video* ADRIENNE's *reaction . . . So . . .*

WILLIAM

Would you mind? [*He reveals a small Sony camcorder*]

ADRIENNE

You have already begun, I think – at the museum?

WILLIAM

A small portrait.

ADRIENNE

It's all right. I like portraits.

From this moment, from time to time, WILLIAM *will video parts of the conversation with* ADRIENNE.

WILLIAM

'His work possesses a luminosity. The bodies are not bodies merely, but a landscape of the merely human . . .'

Don't you love it?

'and here, here in the merely human . . .'

Do you think this guy has any idea of the merely human?

ADRIENNE

There used to be a thing – a straightforward American sophistication.

WILLIAM

Where did it go?

ADRIENNE

You tell me.

ADRIENNE *notices that the table has been cleared, but that* BOBBY *has retired without presenting a bill.*

ADRIENNE

Why was there no bill?

WILLIAM

I just . . . arranged it.

ADRIENNE

An expensive meal.

WILLIAM *debates whether to tell* ADRIENNE *the truth. But just for a split second. Then he says proudly:*

WILLIAM

I work here.

He waves EMILIO *and* BOBBY *over to the table.*

WILLIAM

This is my boss Emilio and my pal Bobby.

As he says this, makes introductions: 'Adrienne Mark, my favourite writer.' 'Pleased to meet you,' etc. ADRIENNE *is rising to the occasion.* ADRIENNE *and* WILLIAM *are leaving the now empty restaurant.* EMILIO *and* BOBBY *are in the near distance, happy.*

ADRIENNE

Good for you, William. You are a remarkable young man.

29 EXT. THE WEST SIDE PIERS. DAY.

The conversation continues.

> ADRIENNE
>
> Lesson one: you should never pay for a rich person's lunch.

> WILLIAM
>
> Are you rich?

ADRIENNE *laughs.*

> ADRIENNE
>
> Actually no.

> WILLIAM
>
> That's what I thought. You seem like a worker to me. Nine to five, five days a week. Sometimes six.

This goes right to ADRIENNE's heart. First of all it is true. Secondly it is just what she wishes people knew about her. WILLIAM seems about to say more, but does not. ADRIENNE looks at him. Twenty years ago she would have said 'What are you thinking?' Now, she thinks to say something generous.

> ADRIENNE
>
> You might look me up in Paris. 21, rue de Verneuil. That was the house I grew up in. It's going up at auction, and I am going to buy it. Where do you live?

> WILLIAM
>
> Here in the meat-packing district.

> ADRIENNE
>
> Everyone wants to be working-class – has to have atmosphere.

> WILLIAM
>
> My grandfather was a butcher.

> ADRIENNE
>
> Then you're entitled.

WILLIAM

I think so.

ADRIENNE *muses a moment.*

ADRIENNE

That's interesting. My mother was a dressmaker. A good one. I used to watch her. I think I know how to write a book because I watched my mother make a dress. A dress is made to hang on the human body, but it is a matter of harmony and balance [*pause*], like a book . . . I have enjoyed this.

WILLIAM

I have enjoyed this.

CUT TO: ADRIENNE *getting into a taxi.*

ADRIENNE

In Paris it is 21, rue de Verneuil. Remember.

Taxi drives off.

WILLIAM

I'll remember.

30   INT.   ADRIENNE'S APARTMENT. DAY.
ADRIENNE *enters in high spirits.*

MILLY

What cheered you up?

ADRIENNE *takes MILLY to her study. Suddenly we are struck by the beauty of this room, and we sense how difficult it is for ADRIENNE to leave the workplace where she has worked for many years. ADRIENNE goes straight to the portrait of herself as a child.*

ADRIENNE

Take this, Milly, in remembrance of me, as they say in the church.

The painting is a portrait of young Adrienne in a navy blue and white suit, complete with a hat and white gloves and socks. The style of the painting is very Balthus-like.

MILLY's reaction is immediate. She takes the picture and looks at it carefully. In other words, she is looking at it deeply. Then, as though for the first time, she looks at the other pictures in the room. Then she comes back to ADRIENNE.

> **MILLY**
> It's the best one here.

> **ADRIENNE**
> That's right. By far the best.

MILLY doesn't say a word. She just holds it. She certainly isn't going to let it go. Not knowing what to say she just turns and we see her marching away. Then she turns.

> **MILLY**
> You know, Miss Adrienne, sometimes I think what people don't know about women is just about everything.

ADRIENNE laughs. A wonderful big laugh.

CUT TO: *A few minutes later. MILLY is dressed to go home. The portrait has been wrapped in brown paper. ADRIENNE is watching the evening news. Using a remote, she mutes it when MILLY comes in.*

> **MILLY** (*very serious*)
> You know, Adrienne, I had a hit.

> **ADRIENNE**
> I know, Milly.

> **MILLY**
> 'Ninety Nine and One Half.' That was the name of my hit. I sang backup to Wilson Pickett on that one.

> **ADRIENNE**
> Wilson Pickett?

MILLY

The Wicked Pickett. He was Soul Brother Number Two.

ADRIENNE (*a little shyly*)

You wouldn't sing it for me, Milly?

MILLY

I thought I might.

MILLY *puts her packages down and sings 'Ninety Nine and One Half (Just Won't Do)'.*

Afterwards she picks up her packages, including the portrait.

MILLY

I'm glad you had a good time with that boy. You don't know how hungry they are. You don't know how hungry they are for what you have to teach them.

ADRIENNE *is nonplussed at this. Very seriously.*

ADRIENNE

Thank you, Milly. See you tomorrow.

MILLY

Got to have one hundred.

31 INT. THE APARTMENT. DAY.

Morning. ADRIENNE *in her study making telephone calls, excitedly.*

31A INT. WILLY'S OFFICE. DAY.

PHONE CALL ONE: WILLY KUNST. WILLY *is in his office with the* TEXAN COUPLE. *His face lights up.* ADRIENNE *is saying she will sell the apartment to the* TEXANS. *The* TEXAN WIFE *is wearing Jack Kerouac's cap and she is standing next to him at his desk and we see her reaction.*

31B INT. ELLIOTT'S OFFICE. EVENING.

PHONE CALL TWO: ELLIOTT SPENCER, *Adrienne's ex-husband, in Paris. Show* ELLIOTT *in his Paris office taking the call; face lighting up. There is a photograph of Adrienne on his desk as well as a wedding photograph.* ADRIENNE *is telling him her arrival is imminent.*

ELLIOTT
When you have your flight information, tell me and I'll meet you.

ADRIENNE
I don't want to be met. I want to come into Paris alone.

31C INT. RAYMOND'S PARIS APARTMENT.
EVENING.
PHONE CALL THREE: RAYMOND, *an old lover of* ADRIENNE's *in his Paris flat, his wife* SUZANNE *standing next to the phone.* RAYMOND's *face lights up.* SUZANNE's *expression goes down as his goes up, as* ADRIENNE *tells of her travel plans. Close-up on a calendar next to the phone at Raymond's. One date is already circled. This is the date when the apartment at 21, rue de Verneuil will go up at auction. Maybe show an announcement of the auction lying over the calendar.* RAYMOND *takes a crayon and circles a second date. Then writes 'Adrienne' on the date he has just circled.* SUZANNE *looks at this 'Adrienne' and then up at* RAYMOND. *Then she turns violently away. She stands at a small desk with her back to* RAYMOND. *Then she turns around.* RAYMOND *is still on the telephone, saying goodbye to Adrienne.*

SUZANNE
My mother is going to Biarritz and I think I will go with her for a while.

RAYMOND *puts his hand over the telephone for a second, looks at* SUZANNE *almost with disdain, then picks up the telephone again.*

> SUZANNE

Paris just doesn't suit me just now. Paris doesn't suit me at all.

RAYMOND *hangs up. They confront each other in silence.*

> RAYMOND

Why must you take what is special to me away from me?

> SUZANNE

But you never had it.

32 EXT. CENTRAL PARK. DAY.
ADRIENNE *is returning from a walk. Jaunty, happy, young. She just breezes past the doorman leaving a happy 'Good morning, Sam' over her shoulder.*

33 INT. ADRIENNE'S APARTMENT. DAY.
ADRIENNE *looks for a split second at the buzzer, then just opens the door and dashes in. MILLY is in the living room, not looking happy.*

> ADRIENNE

What's the matter, Milly? Who's dead?

Over MILLY's head she sees the unctuous figure of HARRY BANCROFT.

> ADRIENNE

Ah, Harry.

She too becomes subdued.

34 INT. ADRIENNE'S STUDY. DAY.
HARRY BANCROFT, *rather like an employee of a distinguished funeral parlour, is – in a very circumspect way – giving* ADRIENNE *a lecture.*

BANCROFT

No profession is completely understood. Auction galleries, for instance. People notice the glamour; the high prices. We tolerate it – to a degree it is good for business.

ADRIENNE

Meanwhile, backstage . . .

BANCROFT

Exactly . . .

ADRIENNE

Hard work. Nose to the grindstone . . . [*imitation of theatrical award acceptance*] all the little people.

BANCROFT

In this case, one of the little people has stolen the show . . . has been given the show.

ADRIENNE

Now you've lost me.

BANCROFT

People, Adrienne, are prisoners of their memories. A sunny day in Provence. They are young, they are successful. They call on a great master – Picasso say. The great man receives them; really as a *beau geste* they buy a little something – a plate, or – a plate. In their mind they have a Picasso. In their mind the beauty of their day, memories of their youth, the kindness of the artist himself all run together and somehow increase, in their own mind – the value of the plate they have bought.

ADRIENNE

I bought the plate in Beverly Hills, Harry. It was a rainy day.

BANCROFT

As you wish. Since we are scraping away romance I will tell you that there are times when my life seems like one long rainy day.

ADRIENNE

I'm so sorry to hear that. You have been so bright and cheerful. You must have a remarkable capacity for what the British call dissembling. Forgive me, go on. One long rainy day . . .

BANCROFT

It's not that easy a job, Adrienne. Rich undiscriminating buyers. If it's good work done by an obscure artist, the job is one of education.

He smiles.

ADRIENNE

Noble work, education.

BANCROFT

Underpaid work, education. [*Warming to his theme*] And then there is the third category. What the public wants.

ADRIENNE

Cut to the chase, Harry.

BANCROFT

OK. I'll cut to the chase. First of all, I thought we were friends. Where did that go? Never mind. Professionally speaking, you promised me a free-hand fire-sale so to speak. Everything must go. There are, frankly, two or three things which make the effort worthwhile as far as I am concerned, and I find today that you have given the most valuable of these things to the maid.

ADRIENNE

You are talking of my housekeeper. I'm sorry to find you have so loose a sense of social hierarchy.

BANCROFT (*really stung by this*)

My sense of hierarchy, Adrienne, is not to be brought into question. As to what you gave to your housekeeper, it's what would have been on the cover of the catalogue. Adrienne, we need a front page. Without a front page we don't have a catalogue, and without a catalogue redolent of charm and association, we don't have a sale. You get my drift.

ADRIENNE

I get your drift [*pause*]. Bring me that plate.

BANCROFT, *surprised at this new tone, brings her the Picasso plate.*

ADRIENNE

Now, Harry. I think I will just take this plate to Provence, where it has probably never been, and heap it over with strawberries. You get out of here.

BANCROFT *pauses. He is not used to being dismissed. He leaves and* ADRIENNE *picks up the telephone.*

ADRIENNE (*on phone*)

Willy, darling. No, not going back on my decision. I just wonder if your Texans wouldn't like to buy it all right now . . . Well no, not the manuscripts. Everything else. Except one portrait of me which stays in Milly's hands in Harlem, USA . . . [*pauses while Willy says something like 'Bless You!'*]

ADRIENNE *hangs up.*

35 INT. ADRIENNE'S APARTMENT. DAY.

MILLY *at one end of the table,* ADRIENNE *at the other.*

ADRIENNE *is smoking.*

ADRIENNE

If you were to go into my bedroom, in the chest of drawers, there is a cardboard box. I want to show you something.

We follow MILLY *into Adrienne's bedroom.* MILLY *goes to the chest of drawers and pulls the panel at the bottom. Inside is an old cardboard box. Across it written in script is the name 'Madeleine'. MILLY handles it with extreme care (we have not seen this reverence in her before. Actually, she is almost in tears). She comes back to the dining room and lays it before ADRIENNE. ADRIENNE, with the same reverence, lifts the top from the box. In it are a very few things; clearly, ADRIENNE knows every one. She takes them out. The things are: three sketches of three dresses, a beautiful brooch and a pair of gloves. The gloves are unusual – embroidered with stars.*

ADRIENNE
My mother's brooch – she designed this. And these [*gloves*]. This was what her work was like.

MILLY *doesn't say anything.*

ADRIENNE (*fierce*)
My mother was an artist and a worker. I respect your work.

MILLY
I know.

ADRIENNE
Elliott Spencer, the man I married, told me something once. What Mr Spencer told me is that in the army they have a device to be used at night. Apparently, this device looks into the night and can find any tiny source of light and draw that light in, concentrate it – and one has enough light to read a map by. In America, Milly, you have given me light to read my map by.

The two are silent. MILLY is thinking what she can do to give back to ADRIENNE.

MILLY
And now you go back to find your mamma in Europe.

ADRIENNE
I'm going to try.

MILLY

My mamma didn't like this world.

ADRIENNE *looks up.*

MILLY *(continuing)*

She liked the other world. She liked me to sing just by
myself. I'm more like her now than I am like me.

MILLY *sings 'Will the Circle be Unbroken'.*

MILLY

That one she liked.

ADRIENNE

Thank you.

On ADRIENNE. *She is watching* MILLY *with complete attention.
There are tears in her eyes. We should sense that this is her leave-
taking. The America she has loved.* MILLY *stops, turns around.*

36 OMITTED IN FINAL VERSION.

37 EXT. ADRIENNE'S APARTMENT HOUSE. DAY.
Limo at the curb. WILLY *helping* ADRIENNE *into the car (rainy
day would be best).*

WILLY

You just go. Also you should sell the manuscripts. To the
Texans. [*Raising his voice*] You *need* to sell them the
manuscripts. Make a clean break. What awful advice for
an agent to be giving a writer.

ADRIENNE *gets into the limo while* WILLY *keeps on talking.*

WILLY

They're very nice people. They reverence you. I mean the
Texans. They want to put your manuscripts in air-tight
humidified glass cases where people of West Texas can
see and appreciate. Also, they'll pay through the nose.

By *this time* ADRIENNE *is in the limo.* WILLY *climbs in.*

WILLY
To Paris like Grant took . . . what did he take, Grant?

ADRIENNE
Richmond, darling Willy. Grant took Richmond.

WILLY *shakes his head.* ADRIENNE *and* WILLY *settle into the back seat of the limo.* WILLY *takes* ADRIENNE's *hand. We see the limo drive off.*

38   EXT.   CHAMPS ELYSÉES. DAY.
Champs Elysées; urgent traffic; things happening; business.

CUT TO: *Imposing office entrance. Cut into name-plate of a film company owned by Virginia Kelly. The company is called 'Kelly Productions' and it has a 'class' logo: a château perhaps. VIRGINIA KELLY has been a successful executive at a major American film studio – marketing end – and has now set out on her own. Tilt up to move into windows. VIRGINIA turning away from the window as she speaks.*

39   INT.   KELLY PRODUCTIONS OFFICE. DAY.
VIRGINIA KELLY, *American, mid 30s, is sitting behind a desk bigger than Louis B. Mayer ever thought of.* PATRICE LEGENDRE, *early 30s, is sitting across this desk.* PATRICE, *a bright, glossy young European, partly French, owns the copyright to a film, made by his father,* FRANZ, *which* VIRGINIA's *company wishes to remake. The issue is simple; the film* PATRICE *owns is a New Wave film like* L'Aventura *or* Last Year at Marienbad *in which disillusioned privileged people walk through grand settings.* VIRGINIA *wants the privilege and the settings; does not understand the mental issues.* PATRICE *does not take her seriously. There is more of an attraction on* VIRGINIA's *side. There is something about the aggressiveness in her behaviour that tells us she wants some kind of personal relationship with* PATRICE. PATRICE *thinks he is repelled by her, but, if he were to*

131

be honest, he is attracted to her at the same time. VIRGINIA *is in the process of rejecting a script.*

Various shots of VIRGINIA *and* PATRICE *in their discussion, still unheard by us. But their looks and body language should give us more than an inkling of their relationship. As she tosses the script on to her desk we hear her say:*

VIRGINIA

It's boring.

PATRICE

Then tell me how to fix it.

VIRGINIA

I don't tell my automobile mechanic how to fix my car. I drop it off. He says thank you. I pick it up the next day. It's fixed. If it's not fixed I know it.

PATRICE

You make it sound so easy.

VIRGINIA

Easy as pie.

PATRICE

My father's film was anything but easy. [*In French*] It had to do with the decline of people who had the landscape of old civilization around them but no will to understand or to rule [*he translates this into English haltingly*].

While PATRICE *speaks, the camera may drift over to the poster of* The Friendly Bear *for comic contrast.*

VIRGINIA (*cutting him off*)

Hold on there, junior. You're telling me that that's what *Lola Found Again* was all about?

PATRICE

Yes, I am.

VIRGINIA

Well, let's not remake that movie.

PATRICE

What do you mean, let's not remake that movie?

VIRGINIA

What I mean is that that's not the *Lola Found Again* that I saw.

PATRICE

What's the *Lola* that you saw?

VIRGINIA

I remember a movie about a sexy young girl who disappears in a big old château. When her husband finally finds her, she realizes that she's had enough of him and wants a divorce.

PATRICE

But isn't your reading a little simple-minded? Excuse me. My father struggled to make his movie the way he wanted it . . . the way I just described it to you.

VIRGINIA

Junior, spare me this Oedipal crap. Besides, we're not talking about your father's film. Excuse *me*. We're talking about mine.

PATRICE

Ours.

VIRGINIA

No, mine. If I buy the rights to remake *Lola* –

PATRICE

If I let you buy the rights to remake *Lola* –

VIRGINIA

Listen – I am aiming for more than your typical art house crowd in Paris. I'm aiming for the people in Paris,

133

Texas. You have to think big. Patrice . . . let me give you a word of advice. Go to a video store and rent *Call Me French*. It's a perfect example of what I want you to script for me.

PATRICE

Virginia . . . I have seen *Call Me French*. My father directed it from Adrienne Mark's book in 1960.

VIRGINIA

I'm talking about the American version that was shot here in the '70s, also based on Adrienne Mark's book. [*Curious, for once*] Don't tell me that you know Adrienne Mark?

PATRICE

I've known her since I was a kid.

40   OMITTED IN FINAL VERSION.

41   EXT.   CHARLES DE GAULLE AIRPORT. DAY.
ADRIENNE *gets into a taxi.*

42   EXT.   ARC DE TRIOMPHE. DAY.
Now ADRIENNE *is being hurled through the traffic at the Arc de Triomphe. It is like those bumper cars at an American carnival, with traffic coming at you broadsides, then suddenly veering away.* ADRIENNE *is stoic, the driver nonplussed.*

43   EXT.   ADRIENNE'S TAXI NEAR THE LOUVRE. DAY.
Adrienne's TAXI DRIVER *is a huge man, a kind of brute. He drives with one hand, with little regard for* PEDESTRIANS. *In fact, he talks non-stop.*

DRIVER

I don't know if you know it, Madame, but we live in the last days of pseudo-Democracy.

ADRIENNE

Do we really?

DRIVER

The Barbarians have arrived. And I am prepared! I'm ready for a fight! My vote should be worth twelve of whatever these . . . [*He waves his hand – out the window we see a crowd of* NEW PARISIANS – *people of many nationalities*] . . . In my view one should have one vote for every generation one's family has been in France . . .

ADRIENNE

Back to Napoleon?

DRIVER

Back to Charlemagne! Back to Charlemagne!

The DRIVER, *full of zeal, takes both hands off the wheel. In the process (the taxi is in heavy traffic near the Louvre) he almost runs over a* YOUNG BLACK WOMAN. *He slams on the brakes, and then, most unfairly, begins to shout at the* YOUNG WOMAN *he has almost killed.*

DRIVER (*in French*)

Connasse! Watch where you're going!

Suddenly, FOUR COMPANIONS *of the* YOUNG WOMAN *appear – also black – and run around the taxi. The* YOUNG WOMAN *who was almost struck comes to the open window of the* TAXI DRIVER *and curses him and strikes at him with her handbag.*

ADRIENNE, *now in a fury, gets out of the taxi, grabs her bag and her typewriter – all of this violently – then kicks the door of the*

135

taxi shut – and like a soldier in wartime, picks up her belongings and stalks off. The TAXI DRIVER *curses her.*

43A   EXT/INT.   MILLY'S HOUSE. HARLEM. EVENING.
MILLY *isn't there, but her husband* FRANK *is there and is seated, and so is* HARRY BANCROFT. BANCROFT *seems to have been delivering one of his lectures. The door opens and* JEREMY, MILLY *and* FRANK's *youngest son, enters. He is seven, and carries a skateboard. He is a real fashion plate: sneakers, cap turned backwards on his head, etc.* BANCROFT, *best 'I'm the politest guy in the world' manner, makes a kind of phoney hesitation in his speech.*

> BANCROFT (*to Jeremy*)
> Well . . . what ho! [*To* FRANK *as though they were old friends*] I won't bore you with every single detail but if you cast your eye on the figure I am about to write.

BANCROFT *takes a fancy Cross ballpoint and writes on the back of a business card . . . at which point* MILLY, *arms full of groceries, enters. She looks different in this context – even stronger if that were possible. As we include* MILLY *in the shot we see the portrait of Adrienne on the wall.*

> MILLY
> What's this?

> JEREMY
> We've hit the jackpot!

> MILLY (*to Jeremy*)
> Take these groceries to the kitchen.

Which JEREMY *does.* FRANK *hands* MILLY *the card with the writing on it and nods upwards at the portrait.* MILLY *puts the card down like it was a dead animal and turns politely to* BANCROFT. *The echo of Adrienne should be clear.*

136

MILLY

I want you to look carefully at the things on this wall, Mr Bancroft. This is my mamma [*studio portrait of the 1940s*]. This is when I married Frank [*she gives a certain stern look to Frank*]. This is my son Wayne, my son Darrel, and my son Jeremy who you just met [*no special emphasis*]. This is my friend Adrienne Mark, and this is my gold record [*close-up on gold record for 'Ninety Nine and One Half (Just Won't Do)' sales of more than one million dollars*]. For sales of more than one million dollars. I sang on that with Wilson Pickett. [*To Frank*] Now which one of these do you want me to take down?

A moment's silence.

MILLY (*continuing*)

Goodbye, Mr Bancroft. I'll just show you to the door.

Bancroft exits. JEREMY enters and is silent. FRANK is abashed.

MILLY

Got to have one hundred. And you got to know when you have.

44 EXT. LOUVRE. DAY.

We follow ADRIENNE towards the Louvre. She stands in front of the pyramid, small typewriter case in left hand, bag in right. This is a new Paris, all right. She looks like an immigrant in a new country. Long snaking line of tourists waiting to enter.

FLASHBACK: PARIS, 1936. *The Louvre as it was. Back to* ADRIENNE *in the present.*

137

45 EXT. ELLIOTT'S APARTMENT, PARIS. GARDEN. DAY.

A large, elegant apartment on the ground floor, opening on to an old and charming garden with a stone fountain. The apartment is tastefully cluttered with books, drawings and memorabilia.

> ELLIOTT
> Your luggage arrived yesterday.

There is a clean line-up of ADRIENNE's luggage which she is meticulously counting as the conversation begins. ELLIOTT pours her some champagne.

> ELLIOTT
> Adrienne, you look marvellous.

> ADRIENNE
> I look like an old woman who has been up all night.

ELLIOTT gives ADRIENNE a glass of champagne.

46 INT. ELLIOTT'S APARTMENT. DAY.

> ADRIENNE
> Two minutes into my homecoming in France I am attacked by a right-wing ignoramus who knows nothing. The driver was taking me to my mother's house but I got out and went on foot. Oh, Elliott, do you think I am doing the right thing?

> ELLIOTT
> 'Ignoramus who knows nothing' is redundant. Your English always did come apart at the seams in moments of intense emotion.

> ADRIENNE
> He told me he thought he ought to have one vote for every generation his family had been in France – back to Charlemagne. [*Now reacting to* ELLIOTT's *remark*] My English never comes apart at the seams.

138

ELLIOTT (*recollecting himself*)
Of course it doesn't.

ADRIENNE
You said it did.

ELLIOTT
Well, I didn't mean it.

ADRIENNE
You said it as if you meant it.

ELLIOTT
You are a great writer – acknowledged as such. Please have a little confidence.

ADRIENNE
You always had all the confidence. Even when you were twenty years old interviewing me. Interviewing me. You told me all about myself, I couldn't get a word in.

ELLIOTT
And it went on all day – night and day.

ADRIENNE
You telling me about me.

ELLIOTT
Well, it wasn't only that.

ADRIENNE
No, it wasn't only that.

Almost a romantic moment.

ELLIOTT
There are reams of invitations when you have time for them. Honoured this way. Honoured that. The nicest one so far is this . . .

ADRIENNE (*looking at an invitation*)
Snakes swimming in a polluted riviera.

139

ELLIOTT

Snakes don't swim. And two urgent telephone messages [*handing her the messages*] – you see me, your devoted secretary, how calm I am – Dear Willy Kunst, how on earth have you stood him so long –

ADRIENNE

You're jealous.

ELLIOTT

I am, you see, *I* want to be your best boy now. Anyway, Willy, in *his* best CIA of Old Vienna manner tried to get me to conspire with him to get you to agree to sell all your papers to an attractive couple from Oklahoma.

ADRIENNE (*a little put out now*)

Texas.

ELLIOTT

Same thing.

ADRIENNE

The English have the worst manners of anyone. I loathe the English sometimes.

ELLIOTT

Your look says you wish I were dead or that you were at the Georges V.

ADRIENNE

No, I wish I were dead.

ELLIOTT (*following her, almost to himself*)

Strangely enough, I've been doing nothing but scheming for ways to please you [*taking her hand*].

ADRIENNE

In fact, you've turned down my bed.

ELLIOTT

Fluffed the pillow.

ADRIENNE *rises. After a brief moment they embrace. Then* ADRIENNE *rouses herself.*

> ADRIENNE
>
> Lead me to comfort, Elliott.

47   INT.   ELLIOTT'S APARTMENT. DAY.

> ELLIOTT
>
> There are friends coming when you wake up.

> ADRIENNE
>
> Not too many?

> ELLIOTT
>
> Two. Just two. Franz Legendre and Patrice.

> ADRIENNE
>
> How is Franz?

> ELLIOTT
>
> Shaky, since his stroke.

> ADRIENNE
>
> And Patrice? My God. I haven't seen him since he was two.

ELLIOTT *brings her a folio and opens it. Inside are large prints of very beautiful photographs.*

> ELLIOTT
>
> Like this you mean?

The first photograph is of a young father and a two-year-old son. Behind the father is a cinematographer, a camera and two or three crew members. Clearly, we are on a film set.

> ADRIENNE (*sitting down in a chair and*
> *taking the folio into her lap*)
> Oh, Elliott [*not wanting all her sentiments to show*].

Now ELLIOTT *pulls up a chair and the two carefully take the photographs from the folio one by one. More of the father and son. Others of the father, son, Elliott as a young adult, Adrienne as a young adult.*

ELLIOTT

We've been longing to have you back.

ADRIENNE

It looks so like a family. I'd forgotten.

ELLIOTT

Had you? I hadn't.

He takes the last photo from the folio. It also shows the father and son. But many others – and in this one Adrienne (young adult) and Elliott (young adult) are front and centre. It is their wedding picture.

ADRIENNE

We look perfectly beautiful.

ELLIOTT

We were perfectly beautiful. [*He kisses her hair*] You taught me so much.

ADRIENNE

Among other things how a young man can steal the heart of a vulnerable woman.

ELLIOTT

You are not a vulnerable woman.

ADRIENNE

I was, and am vulnerable.

48   INT.   ELLIOTT'S APARTMENT. EVENING.
PATRICE *and* FRANZ *arrive.* PATRICE *is leading* FRANZ *into the room. He walks with great awkwardness.* PATRICE *supports his arm with one of his. His other arm is around his father's*

shoulders. *Entering the room, FRANZ must look down at his feet in order not to mis-step. Perhaps he must come up one or two stairs very carefully. Then he steadies himself like the great gentleman he is, and assumes a familiar stance, gained from a lifetime of entering important rooms.*

PATRICE *stands back, releases his father.* ADRIENNE *is standing a little in advance of* ELLIOTT. FRANZ *takes one look at* ADRIENNE – *thinks of the changes in her – and also in himself, and falters.* ADRIENNE *immediately comes forward and hugs him.*

ADRIENNE
My dear Franz, how I've missed you.

FRANZ *loses his carefully won composure. He lowers his head. His face is full of emotion ready to burst.* PATRICE *puts his arms around him again.*

CUT TO: *A few minutes later. A* SERVANT *is seating* PATRICE *and* FRANZ. FRANZ *tries to tell the servant to push his chair closer to the table, but stutters hopelessly.* PATRICE *speaks for his father (in French).* FRANZ *says in French, 'No, too close' or 'a little to the right, please', and* PATRICE *interprets until* FRANZ *is placed the way he wants to be.*

ADRIENNE *has time to whisper to* ELLIOTT *before they go to the table.*

ADRIENNE
I am very shocked . . . And is Patrice just dedicating his life to Franz?

There is no time for ELLIOTT *to answer. It is time to go to the table. Close-up on* ADRIENNE's *serious look as* ADRIENNE *and* ELLIOTT *join* FRANZ *and* PATRICE.

ADRIENNE (*now at the head of the table*)
You wouldn't believe the changes in America, Franz.

143

ADRIENNE *is silent for a moment.* FRANZ *looks up.* ADRIENNE *sees that* FRANZ *is unable to respond, so she goes on.*

> ADRIENNE
> People talk about the violence or the drug traffic, but it's not only that. Something just went. Some marvellous simple things we all loved but didn't understand went before we got to understand it.

> PATRICE
> I am afraid they are changing here as well.

Again, the whole table is silent to give FRANZ *a chance to say something, but he cannot.* ELLIOTT *breaks the silence.*

> ELLIOTT
> Patrice is doing the most remarkable thing. He has gone into the lion's den with *Lola Found Again*.

Hearing the name of his most famous film, FRANZ *rouses himself and looks directly at* ADRIENNE *in a kind of horror. His look says, 'It's true. It's true.'*

> ADRIENNE (*to* FRANZ)
> Your marvellous film . . .

> ELLIOTT
> . . . is about to be remade for better or for worse.

CUT TO: *The table towards the end of the meal.* FRANZ *has hardly touched his food.* PATRICE *has just brought up the subject of* Lola Found Again.

> PATRICE
> So every day I talk to this person trying to get her to understand what *Lola* is about. She thinks she is Lola. Also she thinks she understands *Call Me French*. I use your name as a weapon.

144

ELLIOTT (*reading her mind*)
Yes, Adrienne. Franz and Patrice are asking you to do something. To steer her on to the right track, if there must be this beastly remake. You are the only person who can do it.

ADRIENNE
Is it absolutely necessary that there be a remake of *Lola*?

PATRICE
Yes. I'm afraid the issue is money.

FRANZ *cannot allow himself not to speak. He summons all his energy.*

FRANZ (*in French*)
For my care.

ADRIENNE *takes her chair and moves it next to* FRANZ. FRANZ, *because of the shaking of his hand, has not been eating – there is just a small, tactful amount of food on his plate.* ADRIENNE *pushes her plate away. She takes* FRANZ's *hand. There are tears in* FRANZ's *eyes.* ADRIENNE *nods to* ELLIOTT *and* PATRICE *as if to say please continue eating, which they do.*

CUT TO: *The end of the evening.* ELLIOTT, *now, is helping* FRANZ. *This leaves* PATRICE *an opportunity to talk to* ADRIENNE *about Virginia Kelly.*

PATRICE (*laughing*)
[*In French*] She is a beast. Something from beneath the earth in a red dress. One deals with her through her obsessions. She thinks they are her emotions. I have seen her happy only once, and that is when I said I knew you.

ADRIENNE (*looking at* ELLIOTT *and
especially at* FRANZ)
I will see what I can do.

49 INT. ELEVATOR – FRANZ'S BUILDING. NIGHT.

It is an incredibly small elevator – with room for one person only. FRANZ is exhausted. PATRICE must steady him, close the accordion-like doors, etc.

Intercut: FRANZ in the elevator; PATRICE running up the stairs. FRANZ is exhausted and impatient – that shows on his face. PATRICE has been stretched to the limit. He is breathing hard. He pauses to catch his breath.

PATRICE is turning into an old man.

50 INT. FRANZ'S APARTMENT. NIGHT.

Outside the Legendres' apartment. Once again PATRICE must steady FRANZ, operate two double-locks to get in, etc.

Once inside the apartment, FRANZ regains some of his composure, just enough to begin a complaint (the following exchange is in French).

> FRANZ
>
> These things –

> PATRICE
>
> Which things – ?

> FRANZ
>
> That cursed elevator.

> PATRICE (*a little annoyed*)
>
> Better than stairs –

> FRANZ
>
> Not better than stairs – not an improvement –

> PATRICE
>
> Better for you.

FRANZ is taken aback by this. Of course PATRICE means that he, Patrice, is able to use the stairs with perfect ease. FRANZ suddenly takes that meaning. He says 'Hunh – ', turns away from PATRICE and stumbles, barely averting a fall, grabbing on to a chair. PATRICE holds him.

146

FRANZ
Take me to my room – and go.

51   INT.   FRANZ'S BEDROOM. NIGHT.
PATRICE *has arranged FRANZ, who has fallen asleep. Suddenly exhausted, PATRICE slumps into a chair. He looks at his father who is snoring – unattractively. He looks around the room. It is a temple to Franz's career. Pictures of Cannes in the 1950s and '60s, etc. Black-and-white photos. Even Burt Lancaster . . . PATRICE shakes his head and we should get the sense of the weight of the past.*

52   INT.   ADRIENNE'S BEDROOM, ELLIOTT'S HOUSE.
NIGHT.
That night. ADRIENNE *is tossing and turning violently. She is having a nightmare.*

52A   INT.   ADRIENNE'S BEDROOM, LARGE PRIVATE
TOWN HOUSE. DAY.
ADRIENNE'*s nightmare. Once again the* tableau vivant *of the birthday party.* JUDITH, *as before, with* SIX YOUNG GIRLS. JUDITH *seems to have noticed* ADRIENNE. *She steps forward out of the tableau. Superimpose* JUDITH *stepping forward on* ADRIENNE *in her bed. Back to* JUDITH. *She is trying to say something to* ADRIENNE. *We can't hear what she is saying.* JUDITH, *almost insistent, steps forward more and speaks again. Again, we cannot hear what she is saying.*

JUDITH *disappears. One of the* YOUNG GIRLS *steps forward. Show* ADRIENNE *in her bed, very restless now. Back to the* YOUNG GIRL.

YOUNG GIRL
She was saying that if you had wanted to, you could have saved her.

52B   EXT.   COUNTRY. NIGHT.

YOUNG ADRIENNE *escapes. She runs down the road. She comes to the town house. She sees the* FRENCH MILITIA *are taking her mother away.*

52C   EXT.   TOWN HOUSE, 21, RUE DE VERNEUIL. NIGHT.

We are at the town house on the night Adrienne's mother was taken away by the SS guard and the French militia. ADRIENNE *is at the door of the apartment. She trembles, almost lacking the courage to cross the threshold. We hear sounds of heavy jackboots on the steps. The sound is ominous, and contrasts with the dead still of the apartment.* ADRIENNE *glances once around. Then, in a small voice she says, 'Fan Fan?' She says it again – 'Fan Fan?' – but this time in a voice smaller still – she really doesn't want to rouse Fan Fan or discover where he is – or isn't. She strengthens her back – to gain courage. She goes out into the corridor and to the head of the staircase. There, she sees her mother at the bottom of the staircase and she watches as* JUDITH *is dragged away by the SS,* ADRIENNE *runs down the staircase out into the courtyard in time to see* JUDITH *disappear through the big gates.* ADRIENNE *breaks into a run. When she reaches the gates, the* CONCIERGE *grabs her. While the* CONCIERGE *holds her,* ADRIENNE *looks out into the dark street.*

52D   INT.   TOWN HOUSE. DAY.

On her way to the film studio, ADRIENNE *stops to look at the large town house where she grew up. She walks in the courtyard, looks at the ground-floor shops, up at the noble façade.*

53   INT.   OFFICES OF A FILM STUDIO. DAY.

ADRIENNE *is wearing a red dress.* VIRGINIA KELLY *is showing her posters of all her hits. Also a slew of awards.*

> VIRGINIA
> Three hundred million dollars for *The Friendly Bear.* Have you seen it?

ADRIENNE

Not that I can remember.

VIRGINIA looks at her oddly. She is not insulted by ADRIENNE's irony; she is simply thinking, 'How can she not have seen The Friendly Bear?'

VIRGINIA

Three hundred million dollars. We've done so well in round one that we can sell the video for nothing. Of course videos cost nothing so it's volume we want.

Continues the walk past the posters.

Tie-in with *Smokey the Bear*, tie-in with *Grandpa Grizzley* which was huge for us. We *own* bears, the concept of bears, very satisfying.

ADRIENNE

I'm floored.

On poster for a small animated feature — it looks interesting.

ADRIENNE

What is this one?

VIRGINIA

A little girl alone in a big house. Nothing, *nada* and *rien*. Drudgery from my point of view . . . Let me show you what I have in mind for *Lola*.

She pulls down a chart. Then another, then another, like window blinds. One chart says 'Europeans who have been influenced by television'. Another says 'Europeans who can be influenced by television'. The third says 'Europeans who love quality movies'.

'Now, here is Europe today. We don't have anyone who falls outside these three groups. Either they are already hooked by TV or they can be hooked by TV or they love quality films. Patrice doesn't get this. He just doesn't get it. This is what I'm proud of. We took three years — I took three years – to come up with this. If you make a film that appeals to Group One – the already hooked on TV group – and use brilliant material from Group Three – the quality film group – you will get the ready to be hooked on TV group. The secret agenda is to get Group Two into the theatres. What do you think?

ADRIENNE
I will have to think about what I think.

VIRGINIA
But you did it. That's what you already did. *Call Me French* is my favourite film. I watch it again and again.

ADRIENNE
You do?

VIRGINIA
You see, you changed demographics forever. You took people who were reading books and took them away from books and into film – forever.

ADRIENNE
Is that what I did?

VIRGINIA
You bet you did. You changed the world. Now I want you to help me get Patrice on the right track with *Lola*.

ADRIENNE
Yes . . . where is Patrice?

VIRGINIA
Downstairs in the screening room. I have a little surprise for you.

ADRIENNE (*wary*)
A surprise?

VIRGINIA
Before lunch, I'd like to show you my favourite scene from *Call Me French*.

26

27

28

29

30

31

32

33

34

36

37

38

39

40

43

44

46

47

ADRIENNE
Couldn't you just tell me which one it is?

VIRGINIA
Of course I could, but it will show you how I want to attack *Lola Found Again*. I tell everyone I want to do it in the style of Adrienne Mark. Adrienne, tell us how to make *Lola*. You are a marketing genius. Please, please, I'm down on my hands and knees.

ADRIENNE
That I'd like to see.

54   INT.   THE STUDIO. A SCREENING ROOM. DAY.
ADRIENNE *and* VIRGINIA *take their seats*. PATRICE *has joined them and sits in the row behind*.

VIRGINIA
Roll 'em.

The film starts; and to ADRIENNE''*s astonishment, it is the Hollywood remake that fills the screen*.

ADRIENNE *whispers to* PATRICE *(in French)*:

ADRIENNE
Don't tell me we're watching the remake!

PATRICE
This is the version she likes. Hadn't you understood?

ADRIENNE
No, I hadn't . . . but I should have.

CUT TO: *Screening room some time later*. ADRIENNE, VIRGINIA, PATRICE *as before*. *We are watching a scene from* Call Me French, *the Hollywood version*.

54A   INT.   LUXURIOUS APARTMENT. CALL ME FRENCH – REMAKE. DAY.

We are in the living room of a luxurious apartment, 1970-style
'modern', with terrible luxurious touches – a huge picture window
with a panoramic view of the Seine. FRANCINE is sitting alone on
a big long couch in front of the picture window. She is perfectly
coiffured – Hollywood starlet – even Sandra Dee type. Pull back to
show BEN and FRANK mixing cocktails at the bar. BEN is the
dark-haired man. FRANK is the Kris Kristofferson type. FRANK
approaches the couch carrying two exotic drinks in his hand.

FRANCINE

Oh! What's this drink?

BEN

It's called 'Rocket's Red Glare', Francine.

FRANCINE

You know, my real name is Francine, but my friends call
me France.

BEN

I'll just call you French.

FRANK now approaches the couch. Also carrying two exotic
drinks, meaningfully, FRANK puts down one of these drinks right
next to the one BEN gave her. The drinks should really be luscious
looking, and the glasses are close enough together to touch . . .
while FRANK is putting his drink on the table in front of
FRANCINE, and looking her straight in the eye, BEN is slithering
his way right up next to FRANCINE.

FRANCINE

Ooh! Two drinks! What's this one called?

FRANK

'Twilight's Last Gleaming'.

FRANCINE

I just love twilight.

BEN

Hey! What about the 'Rocket's Red Glare'!

152

Close-up on VIRGINIA's *face. This is how she sees herself – a really irresistible girl who is on to how the boys play the game, but she plays it better. Back to the screen –* BEN *seems to have put his hand on* FRANCINE's *leg. The rest of the scene takes place within that context.*

FRANCINE

Who named the drinks?

FRANK

Francis Scott Key.

FRANCINE

Who's he?

BEN

He wrote the National Anthem.

FRANCINE

Oh.

BEN (*his hand has now moved very far up*
FRANCINE's *leg*)

Frank's an author too.

FRANCINE

Oh! [*It is clear that her response is mostly sexual*]

FRANCINE (*to* FRANK)

Oh, are you an author?

FRANK (*his hand moving further up her leg.*
He savours each inch)

Yeah, and you're the kind of blank page I like facing every day.

FRANCINE

I hope you don't ever get writer's block.

FRANK

I've never had that kind of problem . . . as an author.

She lays her hand on his fly.

> FRANCINE
>
> This is some book.

> FRANK
>
> Yeah. It's what you call a good read.

CUT TO: ADRIENNE, *whispering into* PATRICE's *ear* (in French):

> ADRIENNE
>
> I never wrote one word of this dialogue. They brought in someone else after me. But I must admit, it has its charm.

CUT BACK TO MOVIE: BEN *now moves his lips to* FRANCINE's *ear and whispers something in it. We do not hear what he says.*

> FRANCINE
>
> Yes! Yes! YES!

Three big heads fill the screen.

55 INT.   A RESTAURANT IN THE STYLE OF THE
BELLE EPOQUE. DAY.
Forty-five minutes later. Of course, this restaurant will remind us of Maxim's; perhaps it is Maxim's. In any case the scene is parallel to the 1943 flashback in which Adrienne's mother signs away her apartment to Fan Fan, but now, it is not Fan Fan or any comtesse who holds centre stage, but ADRIENNE. We see Adrienne in this scene inhabiting a grand manner she never had before or ever has again in this film. She has arranged the lunch, she has talked to the MAITRE D' – she has in fact played the celebrity card. She enters, PATRICE and VIRGINIA behind her. The MAITRE D' greets her, she gives her name, and his face immediately brightens. He waves his arms alerting waiters, etc. ADRIENNE, PATRICE and VIRGINIA march to a table.

CUT TO: *Half an hour later.* WAITERS *not only hover, they each come to pay special attention. Lots of special orders for special treats. 'Would you like so-and-so, Mme Mark?', 'Mme Mark, the so-and-so, if I may recommend it', etc. To each of these attentions ADRIENNE gives an affable grand response. This just happens to be something she knows how to do; the good part of her heart-wrenching early training. A front office type comes and presents the compliments of the house. 'Bienvenue à France', etc. In a low, but quite audible voice he directs that all the wine and champagne (and brandy, if any) shall be compliments of the house. All this is pure theatre done by ADRIENNE in PATRICE's interest and to make the largest possible point to VIRGINIA.*

CUT TO: The end of the meal. The table filled with food, wine glasses, bottles of wine which have been chosen each one to go with each delicacy, and an empty bottle of champagne. A WAITER comes and clears the things away. ANOTHER WAITER follows with a tray of luscious desserts. ADRIENNE has not given an inch. She is still every inch the grand lady. Suddenly, she is a severe grand lady – a kind of killer going in for the kill.

VIRGINIA

I want it to be big . . . have bigness. You know what I mean. It's all about scale. Scale.

ADRIENNE

Bigness. Bigness and scale.

VIRGINIA (*excited*)

The great thing about you, Adrienne, is that you gave them a work of integrity, you know, a work of art that the Studio knew how to blow up. You have to have that thing, a foundation to build on. I've studied it.

ADRIENNE

You know, it's very interesting what you seem to be saying, but I'm not sure I know *exactly* what you *are* saying.

PATRICE

I'm not sure you want to know.

155

VIRGINIA (*perfectly straightforward*)
I'm saying without something to exploit you don't have anything to exploit.

ADRIENNE
Now I do know what you are saying.

PATRICE
I told you you didn't want to know.

VIRGINIA
I just love it when Sally says 'Yes! Yes!' Of course she had to have two men to get her to that 'Yes!' That's *one* thing I argue with Patrice about. I want *Lola* to have *a dozen* men.

ADRIENNE
In the original film, and in the 'international best-seller' upon which it was based, there were – two women and one man.

VIRGINIA
Oh, I didn't know that. To tell you the truth, I've only seen the remake.

ADRIENNE *smiles. Her smile says 'I might have guessed.'*

VIRGINIA
Anyway, it's better that women do the choosing.

ADRIENNE
Better from a marketing point of view.

VIRGINIA
Much. Adrienne, think what you can do with *Lola*. She was little then and they loved her. But together we can make her big!

ADRIENNE
I have a great title for your remake. Tell me whether it's marketable.

VIRGINIA

Shoot.

ADRIENNE

Lola Found Again . . . Again.

PATRICE *smiles wryly at* ADRIENNE. VIRGINIA *looks perplexed. Seeing him do so, she understands that* ADRIENNE *is joking.*

VIRGINIA

Ha! Gallic wit! I love it! I want it. Lots of it. So, Adrienne, will you hop on the bandwagon with us?

She puts her hand on PATRICE's. ADRIENNE *notices this. As soon as* VIRGINIA *realizes what she has done, she removes her hand.*

VIRGINIA

We're asking you to work on the script for *Lola.*

ADRIENNE

Script doctor I'm not. Marketing genius, *si*. Script doctor, no. I don't think I can help you. But the two of you do have my blessing. *Encore du champagne . . .*

VIRGINIA

I think I've had enough.

Now ADRIENNE *leans forward to* VIRGINIA *and speaks simply in her own voice.*

ADRIENNE

But *I* haven't had enough.

On ADRIENNE *and* VIRGINIA. VIRGINIA *looks a very little bit like the* YOUNG GIRL *in* Call Me French. ADRIENNE *looks a lot like* THEODORE.

56 EXT. PATRICE'S CAR. DAY.
PATRICE *and* ADRIENNE *driving to Elliott's apartment in Patrice's car.*

ADRIENNE

I like her. I like her a lot more than you think I do.

PATRICE

You do?

ADRIENNE

I do. And so do you.

PATRICE

So do I what?

ADRIENNE

Like her a lot more than you think you do.

56A EXT. PATRICE'S CAR. DAY.
PATRICE *pulls up in front of Elliott's house. She kisses him goodbye.*

ADRIENNE (*in French, as she is leaving the car*)
You know, she's a lot more malleable than you think.
Bring her around to the tour of my mother's house. We'll
keep working on her.

57 INT. ELLIOTT'S APARTMENT. ADRIENNE'S
BEDROOM. NIGHT.
*Once again, ADRIENNE has had a nightmare. Once again, she
awakens not knowing quite where she is. Automatically, she looks
around her bedroom to reassure herself, but of course it is not the
same room. On ADRIENNE as she tries to settle her mind and
return to sleep.*

58 EXT. ADRIENNE'S APARTMENT. DAY.
ADRIENNE, ELLIOTT *and* RAYMOND *outside 21, rue de
Verneuil.* PATRICE *and* VIRGINIA *arrive. A POLICE OFFICER
and ESTATE AGENT are waiting to let them in.*

58A INT. ADRIENNE'S APARTMENT. DAY.

Almost silently, out of respect for ADRIENNE, the group tours the building. RAYMOND and ELLIOTT wander through the apartment. As they do they encounter two groups of prospective buyers. A RICH GERMAN COUPLE with an AGENT and a NEWLY RICH FRENCH COUPLE. RAYMOND and ELLIOTT are drawn into their own thoughts as they look around, but not so these others who are obviously interested only in the economics of the transaction. Each group speaks in its own language, perhaps they might speak as follows:

FRENCHWOMAN

This is exactly what we're looking for, but the kitchen is a nightmare.

GERMAN MAN

This is a very noisy corner. The buses stop at that light just down there. We'll have to put in triple glazing to muffle the sound.

GERMAN WOMAN

We can sell it to an American. They're used to noise. But we'll need to build in closets. These old houses never have any.

The apartment seems frozen in time, and looks like nothing has changed since the 1940s.

ADRIENNE enters for a moment. ELLIOTT and RAYMOND fall silent. ADRIENNE wanders off. We hear 'Lieder' sung by Barbara Hendricks.

RAYMOND

Her mother had quite an 'avant-garde' taste . . . I mean, this mix and match of styles, it must have seemed odd at the time . . . If it weren't for the TV set, you'd really think nobody has lived here since Adrienne's mother left . . .

While RAYMOND is speaking, ELLIOTT wanders off to look for ADRIENNE.

159

RAYMOND (*continuing*)
He didn't have the money to change anything after the War . . .

Enter ADRIENNE. She is a little sad. The place is of course not as she remembered it. It is tattered, dusty. Perhaps she shakes her head a little.

ADRIENNE
Look!

She takes ELLIOTT and RAYMOND to a corridor where there is wallpaper in the Oriental mode.

ADRIENNE
I stood here for hours when I was young.

We look at the corridor – Oriental wallpaper. Chinese emperors.

58   INT.   THE DINING ROOM. DAY.
PATRICE is looking at a book of reproductions. VIRGINIA comes and looks over his shoulder. He is a little uncomfortable, but permits it.

VIRGINIA
Find me in it.

PATRICE
What?

VIRGINIA
Tell me which animal I am.

PATRICE closes the book and walks across the room. ADRIENNE passes by the door and looks in. PATRICE gives her a pitiful look.

VIRGINIA (*to ADRIENNE*)
I love your house. It's very 'Cocteau'.

PATRICE shudders. ADRIENNE passes by the door.

VIRGINIA
What's wrong with you?

PATRICE
It just doesn't happen to be very 'Cocteau'.

VIRGINIA
I think it is.

PATRICE
It wouldn't matter, I suppose, what Cocteau would have
thought about it.

VIRGINIA
Of course it doesn't matter. In my mind Cocteau thinks
just exactly what I want him to think.

PATRICE *raises his voice.*

PATRICE
You're stupid. Find what kind of animal you are in the
book. I'll tell you – it's the stupid animal!

CUT TO: ADRIENNE *in the corridor. She hears this last speech
of* PATRICE's *quite distinctly, and then the babble of a continuing
fight.*

59 INT. TOWN HOUSE. DAY.
We flash back to the building 1943. ADRIENNE, *age eleven, in
this same corridor. She is beautifully dressed in costume for an
elegant children's party. She is overhearing a fight between*
FAN FAN *and her mother,* JUDITH, *in the same room where*
PATRICE *and* VIRGINIA *are now. It is a threatening indistinct
babble, except that, quite clearly, she hears the words 'Don't ever
say that to me!' spoken by her mother.*

59A THE DINING ROOM. DAY.

VIRGINIA (*beside herself, screaming*)
DON'T EVER SAY THAT TO ME!

Now VIRGINIA *catches herself. That is, it is almost as if she had heard the echo of her own voice and been frightened by it. She stops. Her mood crashes from mania to confusion, and then ends in hostile silence. The two look around.* ADRIENNE *is standing in the doorway.*

ADRIENNE
I used to hear fighting in this house and I hated it.

PATRICE
I'm so sorry, Adrienne.

On VIRGINIA *who says nothing, but once again, she looks a little like the* YOUNG GIRL *in* Call Me French.

60   INT.   PATRICE'S CAR. ON THE LEFT BANK. DAY.
A few minutes later. The car is stuck in a crowd. A huge crush of STUDENTS.

ADRIENNE, ELLIOTT *in the back seat.* PATRICE *and* VIRGINIA *in front. They are silent, isolated.* VIRGINIA *breaks the silence.*

VIRGINIA
I just want to tell you how sorry I am.

A moment's silence.

Out through the window of the car from PATRICE's *point of view. The crowd is surging around the car. A* STUDENT *turns and grins in at* PATRICE *and* VIRGINIA. VIRGINIA *looks at* PATRICE. *She is a little scared.* PATRICE, *slowly but insistently, pushes through the crowd and we are in the clear.* VIRGINIA *relaxes (almost as though she had her head on* PATRICE's *shoulder).* PATRICE *relaxes in response to her appreciation of the successful navigation of this crowd. Jauntily, he drives now with his left hand only. Shyly,* VIRGINIA *takes his right hand.*

A moment's silence.

ADRIENNE

How is Franz, Patrice?

PATRICE

Not very well.

61   EXT.   ELLIOTT'S HOUSE. DAY.
ELLIOTT *and* ADRIENNE *walk towards the house through the garden.*

ELLIOTT

Pardon the cliché, but 'you look as if you could use a good stiff drink'.

ADRIENNE

I'll take your cliché, and I'll bid you one higher, 'make it a double'.

While ELLIOTT *prepares the drinks inside,* ADRIENNE *sits on a bench in the garden. The camera rests on her a few seconds before she speaks.*

ADRIENNE

All those people milling about . . . snooping and speculating . . . they all seem to want the apartment just as badly as I do.

ELLIOTT *enters the garden with the drinks.*

ELLIOTT

Oh no they don't.

He gives her a glass of whiskey, which she swallows in a single gulp. He sits down next to her.

ADRIENNE

Of course they do. Their reasons are different from mine, but who cares about reasons? Want is want. In the end, it's just a question of money.

ADRIENNE *pours herself another whiskey.*

ADRIENNE

I can't bid any higher than 8,000,000 francs. If someone else can, I lose. Good God, what got into me. How pathetic . . . how pathetically selfish . . . thinking I could trade in the past 50 years of my life for the first 10. And thinking I was entitled to do so, and that nothing could come in my path or get in my way. Where will I go?

ADRIENNE *is moved – perhaps crying or even laughing.*

ELLIOTT (*awkward*)

You can always stay here. [*Silence, during which* ADRIENNE *says nothing*] Besides, there must be some things worth salvaging from those fifty years.

ADRIENNE *stands up and looks at something in the garden – a flower, a branch, anything. She seems intent on not picking up on* ELLIOTT's *intimations.*

ELLIOTT

You know, your unresponsiveness can get pretty damn tiring. Sometimes I think *you're* the English one.

ADRIENNE

Yes, yours is a thankless role. But don't all editors thrive on thanknessless – thanknessless [*she can't say the word correctly*] on self-sacrifice, dammit. The plight of the ghost writer, no?

ELLIOTT

Oh, I don't mind being a ghost writer of sorts. That's my job. But a ghost husband?

ADRIENNE

Ex-husband. An ex-husband.

ELLIOTT

Yes, I do seem to be forgetting that more and more.

ADRIENNE *smiles and puts her hand on* ELLIOTT's *cheek affectionately. She is wearing the ring he gave her (see Scene 48). Then she turns around and heads back in.*

On her way she says:

ADRIENNE
But you mustn't.

61A   INT.   PATRICE'S CAR. DAY.
VIRGINIA
Would you take me to meet your father?

62   INT.   A HOSPITAL CORRIDOR. DAY.
PATRICE *is with great gentleness opening a door.* VIRGINIA, *again a little like the confused young girl in* Call Me French, *is leaning against the bare white wall of the hospital corridor. She is observing, with a serious look on her face, the tenderness of* PATRICE.

63   INT.   THE HOSPITAL ROOM. DAY.
FRANZ *is sitting up in bed.* PATRICE *sees that he is comfortable. Then he goes out into the corridor to get* VIRGINIA. PATRICE *and* VIRGINIA *at* FRANZ's *bedside.*

PATRICE
Papa, I want to introduce you to Miss Kelly who is the producer of our new *Lola.*

VIRGINIA, *with trepidation, gives her hand to* FRANZ *who holds it.* VIRGINIA *looks down at her hand being clasped by* FRANZ, *on their two hands. This is not something* VIRGINIA *has had any experience of before, and it frightens her.*

VIRGINIA (*whispers*)
This business of real is very scary to me.

FRANZ *does not let go her hand until he wants to. Then he lets it go and he smiles. Then she smiles.* FRANZ *whispers something into* PATRICE's *ear. We do not know what his father has just told him. It remains a secret between father and son.* PATRICE *turns and looks at* VIRGINIA, *as if for the first time. An exchange of looks between* PATRICE *and* VIRGINIA. *Followed by an exchange of looks between father and son.*

63   EXT.   17TH-CENTURY CHÂTEAU. DAY.
PATRICE *and* VIRGINIA *pull up in front of an enormous château.*

                        VIRGINIA
        Oh, I love this place. It's great. Just what we need for
        Lola.

                        PATRICE
        How do you know? We haven't even gone inside yet.

                        VIRGINIA
        I know it's right. I want it. Get it for me.

                        PATRICE
        Just like the Ostrogoths.

                        VIRGINIA
        Who are they?

                        PATRICE
        People who knew what they liked when they saw it.
        Rome, for example.

                        VIRGINIA
        Why thank you, Junior.

                        PATRICE
        I'm not sure it was a compliment.

VIRGINIA *looks perplexed.*

64   INT.   17TH-CENTURY CHÂTEAU. DAY.
VIRGINIA *and* PATRICE *walk through a rather desolate great hall.*

VIRGINIA

I never met anyone like your father. When I am with my
father I can never make sense of what he is saying and he
speaks in quite a loud voice.

PATRICE

You are like that poor suffering girl in *Call Me French*.
You latch on. Isn't that the expression? To the right
things for the wrong reasons.

VIRGINIA

Do you think I have latched on to you?

PATRICE

I hope so.

VIRGINIA *looks up and sees a* SMALL GROUP OF VERY OLD
PEOPLE *entering the gallery. At the same moment an alarm bell
rings. The old people take fright and a* GUARD *enters to clear the
room.* VIRGINIA *and* PATRICE *follow the guard, but turn back
for a moment to look after one* OLD CURATOR. *The* GUARD
calls for the CURATOR *and leads him out. He then returns to*
VIRGINIA *and* PATRICE.

GUARD (*in French*)

Not to worry, only a mistake.

VIRGINIA *and* PATRICE *break into a laugh at the same moment,
like children. They run from room to room. In room one, we find
an old curator studying an 18th-century portrait, not frightened at
all.*

VIRGINIA, *in a light-hearted mood, approaches the curator and
the painting.*

VIRGINIA

I think it is the prettiest thing I have ever seen.

The old curator, just loving her energy, really, says

OLD CURATOR (*in French*)
Yes! Yes!

64A   INT.   17TH-CENTURY CHÂTEAU. ROOM II.
STAIRCASE. DAY.
*In room two, VIRGINIA sees a staircase – grabs PATRICE and
they run down the staircase. VIRGINIA leads PATRICE on what
amounts to a sexual hide and seek through several grand rooms –
at one moment hiding at close quarters from a guard.*

PATRICE
You're the prettiest thing I've ever seen.

*A really intense embrace, they kiss. They push open the next door
and . . . they find themselves in the middle of a wedding party
being held in a splendid garden of the château.*

*The next scene is almost without dialogue, but not without sound.
The band playing for the wedding party is loud and bouncy.
VIRGINIA simply swirls through the party. This is something she
knows how to do. Someone asks her to dance – someone else cuts
in and in no time she is dancing with an OLDER MAN who is
obviously important in the wedding party. The band stops the
dancing music and plays some march-tempo music which says 'to
the tables' and PATRICE finds that everyone is checking place-
cards, etc. – everyone but him. He is confused, alone and jealous.
VIRGINIA comes by with the distinguished OLDER MAN. She
whispers to PATRICE.*

VIRGINIA
They need me at the head table.

CUT TO: *The head table. VIRGINIA next to the FATHER OF
THE BRIDE. PATRICE taps VIRGINIA on the shoulder.*

PATRICE
May I see your invitation?

VIRGINIA *laughs.*

We stay with her – then they go to another part of the grounds, perhaps a medieval ruin. PATRICE is ebullient. VIRGINIA is just a little more serious.

PATRICE

But why worry? Ostrogoths to Clovis to Capets, Valois, Bourbon, Revolution, Bourbon again . . .

He does a little dance for her, in front of her, challenging her not to be in a good mood.

And I'm still here!
And don't forget the Inkspots.

VIRGINIA

The Inkspots?

PATRICE

Oh yeah, they're great. Greater than Ostrogoths – the Inkspots.

He sings her a song by the Inkspots.

65   EXT.   PARIS. DAY.
Sign 'rue de Verneuil.' WILLIAM O'HARA is looking for Number 21. He has two pieces of luggage with him – backpack and a camcorder. It seems that he has come directly to rue de Verneuil from the airport.

He finds Number 21, goes in through the courtyard and cannot believe the atmosphere of the cobblestoned courtyard and the creeping vines on the town house.

On the CONCIERGE, an elderly Frenchwoman. See WILLIAM from CONCIERGE's point of view.

WILLIAM senses he is being observed, approaches the FRENCH-WOMAN. (In French – WILLIAM's French is serviceable.)

FRENCHWOMAN
May I be of service?

169

WILLIAM
Mrs Mark, please.

FRENCHWOMAN
There is no one here by that name, sir.

WILLIAM
Adrienne Mark.

FRENCHWOMAN
No, sir. But I have a nice room [*she nods towards his luggage*].

WILLIAM
What?

FRENCHWOMAN
I do not have all day, Monsieur [*nods to sign 'Chambre a louer'*]. Do you want it or not?

WILLIAM
Yes, yes, I do want it . . . Of course!

66   INT.   WILLIAM O'HARA'S CHAMBRE DE BONNE AT 21, RUE DE VERNEUIL. DAY.
WILLIAM's *possessions (camcorder given special pride of place) have been spread around. Now he goes to the window and looks out. He looks out on the paved courtyard where he was standing a short time ago and through tall gates to street.*

67   INT.   ELLIOTT'S CAR. DAY.
The day of the auction of 21, rue de Verneuil. ADRIENNE is in the passenger seat in Elliott's car. The car is stuck in a terrible traffic jam. They are both panicking:

ADRIENNE
You think we'll make it?

ELLIOTT
We still have twenty minutes . . .

ADRIENNE
Will the auction be the way they used to be – the candles –
the rigmarole? Or is it all *La Defense* and Paris of today?

ELLIOTT
The same, but exactly the same. One great candle is lit
throughout. A smaller is lit during the bidding. When it
goes out, a third is lit, and when that goes out – it's over.

ADRIENNE
The old system.

ELLIOTT
But with audio-visual aids – slides. We're here.

ELLIOTT *parks on the side, anywhere, in double line. They run
out of the car.*

68   INT.   AUCTION HOUSE. DAY.
*Inside the site of the auction – Palais de Justice, or elsewhere.
The essential elements are two: the candles (one is always lit –
smaller candles are lit to time-limit the bidding) and the slides of
the apartments for sale. Either an ancient or modern setting will
work. In any case, the PROSPECTIVE BIDDERS (except for
ADRIENNE and ELLIOTT) are in place. We recognize the
GERMAN MILLIONAIRE and the NEWLY RICH FRENCH
COUPLE.*

RAYMOND *is pacing up and down, looking at his watch. The
MAGISTRATES are getting ready to conduct the auction. Perhaps we see the slide projector being prepared; perhaps the big
candle has been lit. RAYMOND looks at his watch. ADRIENNE
and ELLIOTT enter. RAYMOND dashes to his assistant who,
like a dresser at a theatre, helps RAYMOND make a quick change
into his lawyer's costume. Perhaps we go quickly to the GERMAN
MILLIONAIRE who is also looking at his watch and saying
something in German such as:*

171

GERMAN MILLIONAIRE
. . . The French . . . never on time . . . and so ridiculous this echo of the ancient regime.

GERMAN'S WIFE
. . . Maybe we ought to look in Monaco.

GERMAN MILLIONAIRE
Don't worry . . . It's practically no money . . .

Then to:

OTHER POTENTIAL BIDDER
This delay . . . This fuss. In Switzerland less confusion.

Back to:

RAYMOND *showing* ADRIENNE *to the seat he has saved for her.*

RAYMOND
I thought you had changed your mind.

ADRIENNE
No, I didn't change my mind.

ADRIENNE *and* ELLIOTT *are now seated. She looks everywhere – at the* MAGISTRATES, *at the architecture (if any), at the candles and the slides which have come on at this point. The auction of Adrienne's mother's apartment begins. It is a matter of fascination to* ADRIENNE *to see her mother's house presented in this atmosphere. Her eyes move back and forth between the slides of the apartment she knows so well, and the candles which accompany the bidding.*

The bidding follows. At the end we discover that ADRIENNE *has not in fact acquired the apartment. However, in the meantime something remarkable has happened. Looking first at the slides of her mother's apartment and then at the candles,* ADRIENNE *has gone into a trance. The last slide shown is of the dining room. This slide stays on as the bidding progresses.* ADRIENNE *looks back*

172

and forth between the candles and the slide of the dining room. After a time the candles superimpose themselves and then, in ADRIENNE's mind a tableau comes to life. It is a familiar visual to us from ADRIENNE's nightmares: the birthday party.

JUDITH is lighting candles on a cake. After she has lit the candles, she looks up. It is as though she were seeing ADRIENNE in the auction chamber. Now the ghost scene around JUDITH comes alive, and we see YOUNG ADRIENNE (age eleven) in costume with SIX OR SEVEN YOUNG GIRLS of her age.

> JUDITH
>
> I hope you remember the happy times, because there were happy times in our house. Do you remember your birthday? Do you remember the costume I made for you?

> ADRIENNE (*in the auction chamber*)
> Blue silk.

In the ghost scene YOUNG ADRIENNE is blowing out the candles on the birthday cake.

> ADRIENNE
>
> Can it be that I can accept the happy times for what they were?

> JUDITH
> Yes you can! You must!

Here we return to the bidding (outlined on following pages). Within the context of the bidding:

JUDITH leaves the birthday tableau which fades behind her, and comes down to the front of the row where ADRIENNE is seated. She speaks directly, with an air of command.

> JUDITH
>
> I forbid you to worry. If they touch you I will kill them. If they touch you I will kill them.

The other characters in the tableau fade, but JUDITH does not. She remains alive in ADRIENNE's perception as the auction ends.

RAYMOND *and* ELLIOTT *turn to her. They see her transfixed. She is smiling; let us say a beatific smile.* RAYMOND *and* ELLIOTT *look at each other. We should understand that this has happened before: they have looked at* ADRIENNE *only to discover that she is having a reaction quite different from the one they expected.*

AVOCAT REQUERANT
Il plaira au tribunal d'ordonner la vente du bien saisi pour le compte de mon client, la Banque de Madagascar et des Commores . . .

JUDGE
La vente est ordonée, Maître Rentadour, décrivez le bien vendu.

HUISSIER (MAÎTRE RENTADOUR)
[*On and off with close-up faces of bidders in the audience*] Mardi 2 avril 1995. Vente sur saisie immobilière d'une partie d'un hôtel particulier sis rue de Verneuil, au numéro 21. Le lot comprend au deuxième étage, un appartement comprenant entrée, couloir-galerie, salle à manger, trois chambres, une salle de bains, une cuisine, deux débarras, séjour, salon, dégagement, office et accès, au troisième étage un appartment comprenant une entrée, un séjour, une cuisine, deux chambres, une salle de bains, un débarras, un dégagement; au quatrième étage, sous combles, deux chambres de service, chacune comprenant son cabinet de toilette avec douche et WC, et coin cuisine.

JUDGE
Sur la mise à prix de quatre millions de francs, le montant de frais s'élève a 25 433 28 francs. Les enchères progresseront de cinquante mille en cinquante mille francs.

HUISSIER
Quatre millions de francs. Premier feu!

The first of two small candles has been lit. It burns for about 30 seconds.

The bids immediately escalate: 4.1 million de francs, 4.2, 4.3 . . .
GERMAN MILLIONAIRE, *4.8;* ADRIENNE, *5;* TITAN WITH
MAÎTRE ERTAUD, *5.2;* ADRIENNE, *5.3 million de francs* . . .
There's a pause in the bidding.

> HUISSIER
> Cinq millions, trois cent mille de Maître Cayrol, premier feu.

NADINE *whispers something in* CHARLES-HENRI's *ear*
(MAÎTRE VALVRON).

> HUISSIER
> Maître Cayrol, deuxième feu.

The clerk lights the second candle.

> MAÎTRE VALVRON (*for* GERMAN
> MILLIONAIRE)
> Six millions.

Whispering in the audience.

> HUISSIER
> Maître Valvron, six millions. Premier feu.

The clerk goes back to light the first candle again.

> RAYMOND
> Six millions, cinq cent.

> HUISSIER
> Maître Cayrol, six millions, cinq cent . . .

> MAÎTRE ERTAUD (*for* NEWLY RICH
> FRENCH COUPLE)
> Six millions, sept cent cinquante.

> MAÎTRE VICKS
> Sept millions.

175

HUISSIER

Maître Vicks, sept millions . . .

RAYMOND

Sept millions, cinq cent . . .

HUISSIER

Maître Cayrol, sept millions, cinq. Premier feu.

The clerk lights the first candle.

MAÎTRE ERTAUD (*for* NEWLY RICH
FRENCH COUPLE)

Sept million, sept cent cinquante.

RAYMOND

Huit millions.

MAÎTRE VALVRON

Huit millions, trois.

RAYMOND

Huit millions, cinq.

HUISSIER

Maître Cayrol, huit millions, cinq . . .

MAÎTRE ERTAUD

Neuf millions.

There's a pause.

HUISSIER

Maître Ertaud, neuf millions de francs. Premier feu.

Here ADRIENNE *awakens to discover she has lost her house, the reverie breaks and her descent into the real world is precipitous and devastating. She seems to lose all energy.* ELLIOTT *and* RAYMOND *exchange a look, and with unspoken understanding move to her side.*

69   EXT.   ALONG THE SEINE. DAY.

ADRIENNE *is walking along the quai arm in arm with* ELLIOTT *to her right and* RAYMOND *to her left. She puts her head on* ELLIOTT's *shoulder. This gesture causes* RAYMOND *to free his arm from her.*

> RAYMOND
> You still have ten days to come up with a new bid . . . Of course, it has to be ten per cent higher . . .

> ADRIENNE
> With what money, Raymond? . . . With what money?

A pause . . . They walk a little further.

> RAYMOND
> Are you all right, Adrienne?

> ADRIENNE
> Have I ever been all right?

RAYMOND *tries to think of something to say, but* ELLIOTT *beats him to it.*

> ELLIOTT
> Actually, yes.

ADRIENNE *brightens a little and gives her arm to* ELLIOTT, *a fact noticed by* RAYMOND *who moves a step away.* ADRIENNE *takes her arm out of* ELLIOTT's. *She turns towards both of them.*

> ADRIENNE
> I just need to be by myself.

She kisses both of them and walks away.

69A   INT.   ELLIOTT'S APARTMENT. DAY.
ADRIENNE *is on the telephone.*

> MILLY'S VOICE (*over the telephone*)
> Did you get the apartment?

> ADRIENNE

I didn't get it, Milly, but I have another chance. It's only a question of money. I have to come up with more money.

> MILLY'S VOICE (*over the telephone*)

Wilson Pickett used to have a song. 'Ninety Nine and One Half (Just Won't Do)' . . . Got to have a hundred.

ADRIENNE *laughs.*

> ADRIENNE

Keep me safe, Milly. You sound like Willy Kunst. Goodbye.

70   INT.   A CAFÉ. DAY.

An hour or so later. ELLIOTT *and* RAYMOND *are both a little drunk. One table away is a distinguished, very chic* PARISIAN WOMAN *in her fifties. The kind of woman Paris used to abound in. She eats a sorbet. She picks at it as though it weren't nearly as good as she deserves, her toy poodle looks on greedily, and she feeds the dog a spoonful.*

WILLIAM O'HARA *is walking by the café with his Sony camcorder.*

We see WILLIAM's *strong reaction to the woman. He picks up his Sony . . . Then through the Sony we see the* WOMAN. WILLIAM's *careful framing of the shot.*

To RAYMOND, *looking at* WILLIAM *with sullen disapproval.*

> RAYMOND

I don't like young men.

> ELLIOTT (*looks up at* WILLIAM)

Young man with a camera.

RAYMOND *looks at* WILLIAM.

> RAYMOND

Civilization of *journalisme.*

ELLIOTT

I shouldn't criticize. I was a young man with *pad and pencil*.

RAYMOND

Yes, that's right. [*Realizing he has been rude*] That was hard on me when you came to Paris.

ELLIOTT

With pad and pencil. I was earnest at least. Not just floating around cafés.

RAYMOND

Oh, you floated a little.

ELLIOTT

Not this same discussion.

RAYMOND

But we've never had it?

ELLIOTT

Actually, you're right!

They are silent for a moment. WILLIAM *continues to film.* ELLIOTT *looks at him.* RAYMOND *looks at his drink.*

RAYMOND

I thought I was the better man, you see. Better for her. You dashed in and out and then she dashed out.

ELLIOTT

I think you were the better man.

RAYMOND (*touched*)

I . . .

ELLIOTT

You looked after her.

RAYMOND

Do you remember the day at the pond? When we swam naked?

ELLIOTT
You were the one to suggest it.

RAYMOND (*suddenly animated*)
Not suggest it. Do it! Do it! The first to jump in!

ELLIOTT
She laughed and laughed.

RAYMOND
She is still laughing, thank God!

ELLIOTT *watches* WILLIAM *put his Sony away and leave.*

ELLIOTT
And now I find that my role is essentially protective.

RAYMOND
I didn't mean to say you did wrong, Elliott, only that . . .

ELLIOTT
I used to be an annoying little twit.

RAYMOND (*his first laugh*)
Well, since you said it.

ELLIOTT
But not any more, I hope.

RAYMOND
No, not any more. Partner in crime – the strange crime of
loving Adrienne Mark . . . [*pause*] Spencer.

70A INT. MILLY'S HOUSE IN HARLEM. DAY.
*On a small table there are some knick-knacks and a rather ornate
silver-plated sweet dish. In it is Harry Bancroft's business card.
MILLY looks at this, and turns it over. On the card Bancroft has
written: $25,000.*

70B INT. CHRISTIE'S. RECEPTION AREA. DAY.

MILLY *is in the anteroom with* GIRL (twenty-year-old underpaid Condé Nast assistant type; height of chic). MILLY *looks her up and down.* GIRL *thinks she is dealing with the cleaning lady.* MILLY *just takes the wrapping paper off the portrait and shows the painting without a word. Whole new point of view from assistant.*

70C   INT.   CHRISTIE'S PAINTING STORAGE ROOM.
DAY.
Various paintings hanging on sliding racks. Pop Art juxtaposed against Titians and Rossettis.

> BANCROFT
> . . . tied up. Sorry to make you wait. Work work work.

> MILLY
> Ummm mm.

They're walking towards BANCROFT's *office.*

> BANCROFT
> Oh, that lovely, lovely portrait.

> MILLY
> I want to have it *cleaned.*

MILLY *looks at him slyly. Beginning of negotiation.* BANCROFT *looks at portrait . . .*

> BANCROFT
> Well, it's really quite all right as it is . . .

> MILLY
> I want it bright and shiny.

BANCROFT *becomes a little hostile, as they enter his lavish private office.*

70D   INT.   BANCROFT OFFICE. DAY.

BANCROFT

Well, we don't do that kind of work. I suppose I could recommend the services of people who do . . . [*Suddenly more pliable*] Of course if you ever want to sell it . . .

MILLY

. . . I have a friend, Masters from Harvard, said to tell you she worked at the Fogg, a place called the Fogg. Now she works with kids. She said it was a nice painting. One of the best of its kind . . .

MILLY *leans forward and puts card on* BANCROFT's *desk.*

MILLY

She said you could just add another zero to this.

71   EXT.   TOWN HOUSE AT 21, RUE DE VERNEUIL.
DAY.
ADRIENNE *goes into the courtyard meaning to muse silently; instead she sees* WILLIAM.

WILLIAM (*jaunty*)

There you are!

ADRIENNE

Are you a ghost too?

WILLIAM *looks around at his body; pinches himself.*

WILLIAM

No, not yet.

ADRIENNE

It's been a little strange. You meet a boy in a museum, and he shows up in your mother's house.

WILLIAM

I expected to find you here.

ADRIENNE

And instead I find *you* here.

182

WILLIAM

I hope you're not upset.

ADRIENNE

It's fine, as long as you're not a ghost.

WILLIAM

You said I could come, so I came. No one knew who you were or where you were. One of the most famous women in the world, and no one knew who you were or where you were.

ADRIENNE

And there was a Chambre de Bonne, a Chambre de Bonne, *just for you* . . .

WILLIAM

And I was first in . . . like the Marines.

ADRIENNE *just laughs and laughs. This day has been too much for her.*

72   OMITTED IN FINAL VERSION.

73   NOW 69A.

74   INT.   ELLIOTT'S APARTMENT. DAY.
ADRIENNE *on the telephone to* WILLY KUNST.

ADRIENNE

I mean every scrap.

She listens to WILLY.

ADRIENNE *(a little wicked)*
Including the scraps I wrote to you, Willy. I'm sure the Texans would be interested.

Holds the phone away from her head. WILLY *is objecting.*

ADRIENNE (*continuing*)
Poor Willy. You can keep the ones I signed with love. But
I want top dollar, Willy. Embalm my treasures in the
plastic container!

74A INT. WILLY'S OFFICE. DAY.
WILLY *seated behind his desk, on the telephone with*
ADRIENNE.

WILLY (*to* ADRIENNE)
'Ninety Nine and One Half Just Won't Do' . . . Got to
have one hundred.

Camera pans to reveal MILLY *seated.* MILLY *winks.*

MILLY
Got to have one hundred.

75 INT. CLOSE UP ON AUCTION POSTER. DAY.
An official announcement describes the second sale.

CABINET DE Me CAYROL
AVOCAT PRÈS LE TRIBUNAL DE GRANDE INSTANCE DE PARIS
A VENDRE
SUITE DE SAISIE IMMOBILIÈRE
ET SUR SURENCHÈRE
LE MARDI 15 AVRIL 1995
À L'AUDIENCE DE SAISIES DU TRIBUNAL DE GRANDE INSTANCE
DE PARIS . . . [etc.]

Close-up detail, further down the poster:

SUR LA MISE À PRIX DE:
NEUF MILLIONS, NEUF CENT MILLE FRANCS
9 900 000 F

76 INT. PALAIS DE JUSTICE DE PARIS. DAY.
A candle is lit while the HUSSIER announces:

HUISSIER
Maître Cayrol, troisième feu.

In the courtroom, ADRIENNE *and* ELLIOTT *are seated behind* RAYMOND, *who is standing dressed in his lawyer's attire. This time* ADRIENNE *is taking an intense practical interest in the proceedings.* WILLIAM *is there with his camcorder.*

They're the only bidders present. The candle burns out. RAYMOND *steps forward.*

RAYMOND
Il plaira au tribunal de me déclarer adjudicataire pour le compte de Madame Adrienne Mark, ici présente et acceptante.

JUDGE
A l'issue de cette surenchère, nous déclarons Mme Mark, Adrienne, propriétaire du lot adjugé à Maître Cayrol. L'avocat requéreur ne s'y opposant pas, la propriétaire aura dès ce jour à l'acquittement des frais le jouissance de son bien. Il lui incombe de . . .

The GHOST OF JUDITH *appears and sits next to* ADRIENNE *as if to congratulate her. She takes* ADRIENNE's *hand and they begin to waltz around the room.*

77 EXT/INT.   TOWN HOUSE. DAY.
On a lively French fugue, ELLIOTT *and* RAYMOND *are helping* ADRIENNE *move in.*

They keep coming and going between the courtyard and the second-floor apartment upstairs carrying various suitcases, bags and trunks.

From his upstairs window, a satisfied-looking WILLIAM *watches the scene, observing the process.*

78 INT.   TOWN HOUSE. WILLIAM O'HARA'S ROOM.
DAY.

WILLIAM *comes down with his camcorder.*

78A   INT.   COURTYARD. DAY.

WILLIAM *takes an interest in the moving process. It will be part of his portrait of* **ADRIENNE**. *All at once he is full of energy. Running up and down stairs, filming (with camcorder) from every perspective. On one of these forays he runs smack into* **RAYMOND** *and* **ELLIOTT**. *Bags fly from their hands; one bag falls open and some of Adrienne's belongings fall out.* **ADRIENNE** *appears.*

> ELLIOTT
>
> I'm terribly sorry, Adrienne . . . Clumsy . . . My fault.

> RAYMOND
>
> Actually, this young man's fault.

> ELLIOTT (*to* RAYMOND)
>
> The young man with the camera.

> ADRIENNE
>
> His name is William O'Hara. He is from New York City and he's here at my invitation.

WILLIAM O'HARA *is totally nonplussed. He introduces himself to* **ELLIOTT.**

> WILLIAM
>
> William O'Hara, William O'Hara. Very pleased to meet you.

And **WILLIAM** *goes to* **RAYMOND.**

> William O'Hara, William O'Hara. Glad to meet you.

> ADRIENNE (*to* WILLIAM)
>
> Mr O'Hara, let me take you to dinner. It's my treat, but you choose the place.

79   INT.   A NIGHT-CLUB. NIGHT.

WILLIAM *is taking* ADRIENNE *out for the evening. He has found a place where a* SINGER *from the 1940s entertains. Before this* SINGER *comes out on stage we hear* ADRIENNE *and* WILLIAM.

WILLIAM
This is one of my finds.

ADRIENNE
You are a quick study.

WILLIAM
Very quick. I hadn't much else to do. Find interesting things. Wait for you. And now you are here. And in your home. How does it feel?

ADRIENNE
I didn't know I wanted it so much.

WILLIAM
I wonder what it will be that I want 'so much', as you say.

ADRIENNE
I hope you find it.

WILLIAM
It's about courage isn't it.

ADRIENNE
Yes.

The SINGER *from the 1940s comes out.* WILLIAM O'HARA *takes* ADRIENNE's *hand. She looks at him, he looks straight-forward with utter confidence. She allows it.*

80 INT. ADRIENNE'S APARTMENT. NIGHT.
Upstairs, WILLIAM *edits his videotaped footage of* ADRIENNE.

81 INT. ADRIENNE'S APARTMENT. DAY.
ADRIENNE *has been inspired to do a little physical work on the*

apartment. She has brought a box into the dining room. Out of it she takes a picture of her mother. In this picture, her mother is dressed simply. She takes out a second picture. It is her mother and Fan Fan, dressed in a spirit of conventional elegance. She lays the picture of her mother with Fan Fan aside, almost in disgust. She looks again at the picture of her mother. It is a marvellous portrait in black and white – Cecil Beaton style. She puts it in the centre of the table, with great reverence. Suddenly, without thinking about it (or looking at it), she hurls the picture of her mother with Fan Fan to the corner of the room.

The GHOST OF FAN FAN *appears. He is standing behind* ADRIENNE, *who does not notice.*

On the table next to the box is a brand new hammer and nails for hanging pictures. This is meant to be a kind of homecoming ritual for her. She judges space – where to hang the pictures; where the light will fall. The physical part of hanging a picture is new to her – part of her new life. She puts a nail to the wall. ADRIENNE *takes the hammer back – self-conscious, as though she were pitching a baseball.* ADRIENNE *brings the hammer forward with great force. The hammer hits the nail but the plaster is so weak that a patch of the wall structure is exposed.* ADRIENNE *tests the plaster. She is surprised at how weak it is. It simply falls away. Unconsciously, she removes more and more, as one does picking away a scab. Suddenly a closet under the plaster is revealed. With concentration,* ADRIENNE *continues her archaeology and exposes a hidden closet. She opens the door, and inside is a packet of old letters. She takes the top one.*

At the table she reads the letter aloud to herself with full concentration. As ADRIENNE *does this, the* GHOST OF FAN FAN *moves in front of her. This is the letter:*

ADRIENNE'S VOICE (*in French*)

Dear Otto,

It appears that Judith Mark has been arrested by the

188

French police on Monday night. I cannot imagine that this great fashion designer, a woman whose taste you have often appreciated since she's been a major contributor to the festive lifestyle of all our friends, is being detained as a vulgar Jew. I hope that you understand that I do not defend Jews, only Judith.

FAN FAN'S VOICE *continues*
Jews are other people. As I have often heard you say jokingly to her, when you knew her only as 'Madeleine', 'We may decide who is Jewish and who is not'. In exchange for any help you may be able to supply to our 'Madeleine' – for she will always be so to me – allow me to supply you with the names of a number of exploitative Jews, whose whereabouts are enclosed.

ADRIENNE *puts the letter down on a table. She looks up and sees* the GHOST OF FAN FAN. ADRIENNE *has a perfect calm, but we see a controlled fury under it.*

GHOST OF FAN FAN (*in French*)
I loved your mother and did everything I could to help her.

ADRIENNE
You did *what*?

GHOST OF FAN FAN (*suddenly weak*)
Please, Adrienne. I loved you too. I did my best. It was hard for me too.

ADRIENNE .
Love. I have discovered that weaklings like the word better than any other. You peel it away or you push it and you find something else. Something demonic.

GHOST OF FAN FAN
I was hardly a demon, Adrienne. What did I want – for everyone to be happy, that's all.

189

ADRIENNE
Including the people you denounced to save my mother?
Who were also mothers, daughters, sons, fathers?

GHOST OF FAN FAN
I never sent the letter.

ADRIENNE
So I gather.

GHOST OF FAN FAN
What did you expect? [*He shrugs and sighs*] I know, you
expected bravery.

ADRIENNE
Yes. I expected bravery.

GHOST OF FAN FAN
Well, my dear. You didn't get it.

ADRIENNE *raises her arm and we see the hammer.*

ADRIENNE
If they touch me, I will kill them.

A second later ADRIENNE *is destroying the plaster wall with her
hammer, attacking the* GHOST OF FAN FAN *which disappears.
She goes mad for a time, and then, when this is exhausted, she
pauses a second to catch herself.*

*She goes back to the table. She takes the letter and burns it. She
watches it burn with some fascination. Then, in a mood of trance-
like curiosity, she returns to the closet. Within is an old cardboard
box. She recognizes the box as coming from her mother's establishment, 'Madeleine'. Now, she takes the box with extreme care
to a table. Her hands are shaking. She works with every bit of
energy to control the shaking. She does control herself. She opens
the box and within is the dress her mother was wearing at
Maxim's and also in the Cecil Beaton-like photograph. She
caresses the dress.*

ADRIENNE
William O'Hara! WILLIAM O'HARA!

82   INT.   WILLIAM O'HARA'S CHAMBRE DE BONNE
AT 21, RUE DE VERNEUIL. DAY.
WILLIAM *is trying to edit and organize his film footage.*
WILLIAM *hears* ADRIENNE's *voice calling to him, drops his*
work and runs to her floor.

82A   INT.   ADRIENNE'S APARTMENT. DAY.
WILLIAM *sees* ADRIENNE *about to collapse, but still holding*
the box. His first concern is for her but she says

ADRIENNE
Take the box! Take the box!

With great care, WILLIAM *takes the box from* ADRIENNE *and*
puts it gently on the table. Then he goes over to her and holds her
in a tight embrace.

CUT TO: ADRIENNE's *apartment a few minutes later.*
WILLIAM *and* ADRIENNE *are sitting at the table. Two*
candles have been lit. The dress has now been removed from
the box and hangs from an old hatstand.

ADRIENNE
What they don't tell you is that to return to life is no
easier than to come into it the first time.

WILLIAM *now misinterprets the nature of this moment. He leans*
across the table to kiss ADRIENNE *(of course this too is an echo*
of the crucial scene in Call Me French *and* ADRIENNE *spots it as*
such).

ADRIENNE
No, William . . . I need to be alone now.

Crushed, WILLIAM *gets up to leave. Raymond and Elliott know*
all about this side of ADRIENNE, *but this is his first time. He*

moves silently to the door. Takes one look back at ADRIENNE, *then leaves.*

On ADRIENNE *alone. She smokes a cigarette.*

82B EXT. PARIS APARTMENT OF FRANZ LEGENDRE. DAY.
FRANZ *has come home from the hospital.* PATRICE, *as before, looks after him closely.* VIRGINIA *is with* PATRICE *and now participates in looking after him.*

PATRICE
Are you comfortable, Papa?

FRANZ *tries to speak, but only mumbles.*

PATRICE *brings* VIRGINIA *over to* FRANZ's *side.*

PATRICE
We won"t be gone long. Will you be all right?

FRANZ *tries to speak; cannot, then nods.*

PATRICE *gives his father a kiss on the cheek, and then* VIRGINIA *takes his hand and holds it for a moment before letting it go. They exit.*

82C EXT. PLACE DES VOSGES. EVENING.
VIRGINIA *and* PATRICE *are walking in Place des Vosges.* VIRGINIA *sits down on a bench.* PATRICE *stands in front of her.*

PATRICE
Name?

VIRGINIA
Virginia.

PATRICE
Nationality?

VIRGINIA
American, of course.

PATRICE
Stick to the facts! Nationality?

VIRGINIA
American.

PATRICE
Chapter one in the story of your life?

VIRGINIA *seems very pensive.* PATRICE *speaks for her.*

PATRICE
Patrice approached the bench. He sat beside Virginia, putting his arm around her. Bashfully, he said . . .

VIRGINIA
Yes? What did he say? What did he say? Tell me what he said!

83 INT. RAYMOND'S APARTMENT. EVENING.
RAYMOND, SUZANNE, INTELLECTUAL FRIENDS, *a TV set.*

RAYMOND (*pointing to TV, in French*)
Shall we watch the beast?

A few minutes later. The group is watching the TV. A cultural round-table programme. SIX PEOPLE; among them a neutral-looking BLONDE WOMAN, 35; a TV PRESENTER, about 60 (he is equally 'at home' with architectural, cinematic and political topics) and ACHILLE AYMERIC, a right-wing political commentator. In some ways this man resembles the taxi driver Adrienne had when she first arrived in Paris. He is a big, quintessential Frenchman. His voice is big, low and meaty. He is always saying 'non, non, non', or 'Idiot' as though his word must always be final. He sits like a great lump and although members of the panel are supposed to be equal, the camera and most of the panel members always seem to refer to him. There are two exceptions to this rule, a JOURNALIST *and an* INTELLECTUAL *who look at* AYMERIC *with veiled hostility.* AYMERIC *is talking (in French), followed by the* INTELLECTUAL.

> MAN 1
> She is to France what Moravia is to Italy, what Günter Grass is to Germany.

84   INT.   APARTMENT OF FRANZ LEGENDRE. DAY.
PATRICE, VIRGINIA *and* FRANZ *are watching the same programme. The minute he hears what the* RIGHT-WING COMMENTATOR *is saying,* PATRICE *shuts the set off.* FRANZ *speaks – incoherently, but when he waves his hand it is obvious he is insistent that the television set remain on. We see rising in him a ferocious anger, and we see what* FRANZ *is made of. At first he babbles this next speech, but finally he gets out what he wants so desperately to say.* VIRGINIA *and* PATRICE *are amazed, and look at one another in a way that brings them still closer.*

> FRANZ *(in French)*
> No! Leave it on. We need to hear what he says. What has happened that people like this are even allowed to be on television, that we are subjected to this kind of mockery?

> PATRICE
> I should call Elliott.

> FRANZ
> Yes, do!

PATRICE *goes to the telephone. Sighs. Perhaps he looks up to the wall and sees a picture of* ADRIENNE *on the set of* Lola Found Again.

> PATRICE
> Elliott; it is Patrice. I'm afraid something unpleasant has happened – actually is happening right now . . . [*pause*]

194

Perhaps you should turn on your television . . . the Arts Channel.

CUT TO: *The television programme.*

ACHILLE AYMERIC

You're all getting so worked up about the return of the person you call Adrienne Mark . . . and that I call Adrienne Markowsky.

MAN 1

We're not getting worked up. All we're saying is that she has honoured us by returning to live in France.

ACHILLE AYMERIC

'Honoured'! What has Markowsky done to make herself such a saint? She was born with a silver spoon in her mouth. During France's darkest days, the Markowskys had everything. After the war, she wrote a little book that made her very rich. [*Aside, lowering his tone, but directly into camera*] Some would call that war profiteering. [*Raising his voice again*] And what did she do? She packed her bags and set sail for America, leaving the poor people of France to rebuild our nation while she became a money-making machine, duping her public here and elsewhere.

85 INT. ADRIENNE'S APARTMENT. EVENING.
ADRIENNE *is watching the television programme.*

CUT TO: *The television programme.*

WOMAN

Duping her public?

ACHILLE AYMERIC

Yes, duping her public! Criticizing France from her ivory skyscraper – from the safety of Manhattan. Making money off of our collective guilt, which her writings have done so much to foster. And making money by

195

peddling her twisted version of history to naive Americans, so quick to point a finger at other people while turning their backs on their own miseries at home.

During this diatribe, the TV PRESENTER *has been trying to get a word in. He finally manages to.*

TV PRESENTER
I just want to say that her 'little novel' became a cult book of the post-war youth.

ACHILLE AYMERIC
Not the youth of the factories, or the mines, or the construction sites! Not the youths who were courageously supporting families, putting this great nation back on its feet.

WOMAN (*to* MAN 1, *but so that* ACHILLE
AYMERIC *will hear*)
Who does he think he is? Maréchal Petain?

ADRIENNE *switches the television off. She sits in the dark room.*

86   INT.   WILLIAM'S CHAMBRE DE BONNE. DAY.
WILLIAM *is watching the same programme.*

CUT TO: *The television programme.*

ACHILLE AYMERIC
Oh, shut up! For twenty years now your little parakeet, perched safely in New York, has been criticizing France. Book after book she has spat on us. She advocated a cosmopolitan lifestyle, a pure fantasy accessible only to herself. And now she's come back to lecture to those elected by the French. But there is a limit to how much we can take, that's all. Mrs Markowsky is preaching American solutions, ghettos, lobbies, urban warfare, multiculturalism, and other such rubbish.

196

TV PRESENTER

Gentlemen, please!

MAN 1

France has always absorbed people and will continue to do so, except people like you who put back our progress.

87   INT.   ELLIOTT'S APARTMENT. EVENING.

ELLIOTT *alone in his bedroom. A chance to show something about him and his career. Oxford photo perhaps. Military service. Things of importance behind his cultivated façade. He is crying.*

On ELLIOTT's *TV. The television programme continues.*

CUT TO: TV PRESENTER

Gentlemen, please, gentlemen! Please calm down.

MAN 1

This is a disgrace! He's a fascist!

87A   INT.   RAYMOND'S APARTMENT. EVENING.

RAYMOND, SUZANNE, INTELLECTUAL FRIENDS, *a TV set.*

CUT TO: *The television programme.*

ACHILLE AYMERIC *throws his glass of water at* MAN 1. MAN 1 *responds by throwing water at* ACHILLE AYMERIC.

ACHILLE AYMERIC

We were elected by the populace in order to stop these shit-diggers waking up a past that France has rejected, rejects and will always reject. The *vrais français* are tired of being humiliated.

TV PRESENTER *tries to pull them apart but is unable to. He drags a glass of water from the table and pours it over his own head.*

CUT TO:

RAYMOND
It is shocking.

SUZANNE
I'm not so glad to have Adrienne Mark back in France.

RAYMOND *gets up and leaves the room.* SUZANNE *continues to watch the programme.*

88   EXT.   COURTYARD OF THE TOWN HOUSE.
NIGHT.
We see WILLIAM O'HARA *through the lighted window of his room.* ELLIOTT *runs through the courtyard, and up to* ADRIENNE's *apartment. He pounds furiously on her door.*

88A   INT.   ADRIENNE'S APARTMENT. DAY.
ADRIENNE *is in the darkened room. The TV is still on – but it is another programme. She hears the pounding but is not afraid. She takes one silent moment before opening the door. Almost certainly she is remembering her mother and her mother's words: 'I forbid you to be afraid.'*

She opens the door, and ELLIOTT *takes her in his arms.*

ELLIOTT
That vile pig.

ADRIENNE *collapses into his arms. This is where she is comfortable.*

89   INT.   ADRIENNE'S APARTMENT. DAY.
A month or so later. The apartment has been painted, and otherwise rejuvenated. Fresh curtains on the window. A gentle wind is blowing.

On the table are all the things a writer needs: typewriter, a ream of paper, pencils, pens . . . All, so far as we can see, as pristine and untouched as the newly decorated room.

ADRIENNE *is just getting up from the table. Perhaps there is one sheet of crumpled paper in her hand, which she leaves on the table.* ELLIOTT *enters. He is carrying a newspaper in his hand.*

ELLIOTT
I thought you might like to see this.

ADRIENNE *puts on her glasses, and we see a few lines of a letter Franz Legendre has written about Achille Aymeric's attack on Adrienne.*

ELLIOTT (*reads lines written in newspaper*)
'There are some who are so far below our normal human life that we are shocked into silence when they talk.'

Now we hear FRANZ *speaking the words from his letter.*

Strangely, we who are artists – natural talkers – fall into silence when these strange non-human voices insist on being heard.

90 EXT. A TERRACE OVERLOOKING THE MEDITERRANEAN. DAY.
We look at the Mediterranean, and hear the voice of FRANZ LEGENDRE. *His voice is now very much stronger.*

VOICE OF FRANZ LEGENDRE
But we who are the real talkers also have our powers. We regain them through faith and courage.

Pull up.

Around a table laden with food are ADRIENNE, ELLIOTT, VIRGINIA, FRANZ LEGENDRE, WILLIAM O'HARA, PATRICE LEGENDRE. FRANZ *is standing, reading from the newspaper.*

FRANZ

'To attack Adrienne Mark is the act of a coward. When a person has given you everything and you demand more, that is bad enough. But when all is rewarded by jealousy, then we sink beneath the beasts, because beasts are not jealous. Jealousy and ignorance are uniquely human sins.

'Against these things Adrienne Mark has fought all her life, applying intelligence to what would have otherwise been dark, generosity to what would otherwise have been small.'

FRANZ *puts down the paper.*

The worst thing about these people is that they keep us from our pleasure. To you, my dear Adrienne.

Everyone raises his glass.

PATRICE *gets up and raises his glass.*

WILLIAM *toasts* VIRGINIA.

WILLIAM

In the world of remakes,
Remake life.
Let it flow around you
Up and out
A well-earned shout
Without a frown to hound you.

[to FRANZ]

I want to make a film about you!

FRANZ (*almost the* ingénue)
Oui?

VIRGINIA (*toasting* ADRIENNE)
I came into your house and behaved like a mad rodent.

ADRIENNE (*interrupting her*)
You've already apologized for that.

ELLIOTT
What animal do you feel like now?

VIRGINIA
I have to think about that.

PATRICE
A rabbit.

VIRGINIA
No! Never a rabbit. And I don't like the sexual implications!

PATRICE
But you do like the sexual implications.

ELLIOTT
A doe. She feels like a doe – that's it, no?

PATRICE
Female deer?

VIRGINIA
Jane Doe. That's right.

PATRICE
To my father.

Everyone raises his glass.

VIRGINIA
Well, I'm going to toast the Ostrogoths, and the Visigoths, and the Valois, and the House of Capet – and the Bourbons, our latest dynasty.

PATRICE *interrupts her.*

PATRICE
And the Inkspots, Babe Ruth and the Bonapartes.

WILLIAM *interrupts*.

WILLIAM
And the Bonapartes. And Franz Legendre, again. And
Adrienne Mark, again, and Franz again, and Adrienne
again.

*They are all a little riotous now and everyone has had a bit too
much to drink. WILLIAM clearly has his eye on FRANZ. He is,
quite obviously, even more fascinated by FRANZ, now, than by
ADRIENNE. He has exchanged his camcorder for a small Sony
model, and now he is rushing everywhere filming. Also, he has a
tape recorder. He ends up taking a chair and moving it next to
FRANZ. It is obvious he is going to begin interviewing FRANZ at
his first opportunity.*

FRANZ
A certain amount of humiliation is perhaps good. Life is
bigger than we are, and life demands that we submit to it.
To lose one's ability to speak for a while – well it taught
me that.

ELLIOTT
But it is life we ought to submit to, not other persons.

ADRIENNE
We ought to submit to other persons only in their
wisdom, not their folly.

WILLIAM
And it is the job of culture to help us to know when other
people are acting out of folly – or wisdom.

VIRGINIA
And the old culture is always the best clue to that.

They are all silent for a moment.

PATRICE
I am so glad to have my father back.

Silent again.

ADRIENNE *rises.*

ADRIENNE
Life is nothing but change. And yet, nothing I could keep I kept. It appals me to think of what I had to let go of [*now a slightly lighter mood*]. I always liked the name 'Mark'. My mother's name, I never let it go. Drunk, sober, in Hollywood or New York, with fools or with wise people, I have for many many years been Adrienne Mark. The simple fact is that Elliott Spencer and I . . . have decided to reconnect our lives.

PATRICE
To Adrienne!

VIRGINIA
To Marks and Spencer.

ELLIOTT
To Marks and Sparks.

All laugh. All start chanting, 'Marks and Spencer! Marks and Sparks!' They rise, toast the couple, drink champagne, etc. ADRIENNE and ELLIOTT, bride and groom, pose. WILLIAM records this with his Sony.

ELLIOTT
And so it ends as it began. To my darling and the honour you are to receive at the Festival this evening. With love and laughter. It's a hard pill to swallow being this happy.

91 INT. PALAIS AT CANNES. DAY.
An event honouring writers who have influenced film. ADRIENNE is going up the grand staircase. ELLIOTT, FRANZ, PATRICE, VIRGINIA are following behind. WILLIAM circles around the group videotaping the event; he wears an enormous smile.

Triumphant return to France . . .

A woman who gave so much to the film . . .

92 INT.   THE BRONX. MILLY'S HOUSE. DAY.
MILLY *is watching a segment on* Entertainment Tonight. *A segment about Adrienne.* MILLY *twirls excitedly and cries:*

MILLY
Yes, yes. Oh, yeah.

The Cannes segment ends and MILLY *turns the TV set off.*

MILLY
You got to have a hundred.

93 INT.   ADRIENNE AND ELLIOTT'S SUITE AT THE CARLTON. DAY.
ELLIOTT *is sitting alone at a big round table where we see Adrienne's old typewriter and a pile of papers.* ELLIOTT *is sitting quietly. Once again we sense his remarkable, almost to the point of being annoying, composure. Right now he is toying with the idea. Here before him is some of Adrienne's new writing, but all crumpled up.*

Casually, he moves one or two pieces of the crumpled paper away – as though to make room for his elbow. Then, quite casually, he opens up one of the papers he has moved, and then another. Really, he can't help himself; he is a natural editor. Within 30 seconds he has read four pages, discarded one of these to the floor, smoothed out another and put it in a neat place, found a pen and made some emphatic marks on a third. At this point ADRIENNE *enters.* ELLIOTT *does not notice her. She takes out a cigarette, lights it, and waits until he does notice.*

He looks up. He is utterly unaware (or pretends to be unaware) that he has trespassed. ADRIENNE *doesn't say a word.*

ADRIENNE (*not angry*)
Why go through the trash. You have only to ask.

ELLIOTT (*sighs, embarrassed*)
I'm sorry. I'm so much – the editor.

ADRIENNE
Don't worry, darling, but do leave me alone.

He rises a little stiffly, suddenly, he seems very young as though he were meeting ADRIENNE for the first time – again. He looks at ADRIENNE shyly, and then walks to the door without looking back. We hear the sound of the door closing.

ADRIENNE sits in a chair at the table. Once again she is alone – starting from scratch, or so it seems to her. She looks around the room. There are her bags and Elliott's, a pile of books – some items of glory at Cannes.

ADRIENNE (*v/o*)
One should always be brave on one's own terms . . . At last I am beginning to tell the story. (Adrienne writes) My name is Adrienne Markovsky.

The ghost of JUDITH appears. She is wearing the dress she has always worn in ADRIENNE's dream of her birthday party, and she looks beautiful and strong. ADRIENNE notices her and they exchange looks. JUDITH looks at ADRIENNE with satisfaction and contentment. JUDITH is by the French windows leading to the balcony. She smiles and beckons to ADRIENNE. ADRIENNE rises and walks towards the windows. JUDITH passes between the net curtains onto the balcony and ADRIENNE follows her. We see the harbour and the sea. An image of JUDITH and ADRIENNE waltzing together over the horizon is superimposed on the screen.

Merchant Ivory Productions

Ognon Pictures
&
Fez Production Filmcilik

in association with
Largo Entertainment
Canal+
Channel Four

and with the support of
The Eurimages Fund of
the Council of Europe

present

The Proprietor

CAST
in order of appearance

NEW YORK
Adrienne Mark: Jeanne Moreau
William O'Hara: Josh Hamilton
Willy Kunst: Austin Pendleton
F. Freemder: Joanna Adler
Milly: Nell Carter
Harry Bancroft: Sam Waterston
Texan couple: James Naughton
J. Smith-Cameron
Bobby: Michael Bergin
Emilio: John Dalton
Apartment doorman: Jack Koenig

Guardian angels: Panther, Bull,
                Kim Gilmore,
                Falcon
French ladies: Joan Audiberti,
                Katherine Argo
Woman in park: Judy Alanna

PARIS
Taxi driver: Hubert St.Macary
Pedestrian: Diane Nignan
Elliott Spencer: Christopher Cazenove
Virginia Kelly: Sean Young
Patrice Legendre: Marc Tissot
Franz Legendre: Jean-Pierre Aumont
Raymond: Pierre Vaneck
Suzanne: Guillemette Grobon

THE APARTMENT
French couple: Cherif Ezzeldin,
                Valerie Toledano
German couple: Jorg Schnass,
                Paula Klein
Concierge: Suzanna Pattoni

THE AUCTION
Notaire: Alain Rimoux
Maitre Vicks: Humbert Balsan
Maitre Ertaud: Donald Rosenfeld

FRENCH TELEVISION
French TV presenter: Frank de la Personne
Achille Aymeric: Gilles Arbona
Interviewer: Henri Garcin
Journalist: Jeanne-Marie Darblay

CANNES
Entertainment
Tonight presenter: Catherine Kinley

PARIS 1943
MAISON MADELEINE
Judith Mark: Charlotte de Turckheim
Young Adrienne: Marjolaine de Graeve
Shop assistants: Carole Franck,
Azmine Jaffer
Aristocratic lady: Brigitte Catillon

MAXIMS RESTAURANT
Fan-Fan: Jean-Yves Dubois
Aristocratic man: Herve Briaux

GIRL IN NIGHTMARE
Sophie Camus

'JE M'APPELE FRANCE'
Theodore: Eric Ruf
France: Elodie Bouchez
Nadine: Judith Remy

'CALL ME FRENCH'
Ben: Wade Childress
Franck: Thomas Tomazzewski
Francine: Sean Young

TECHNICAL CREDITS

Production Design	Bruno Santini
	Kevin Thompson
Casting Director	Frédérique Moidon
Costume Design	Anne de Laugardière
	Abigail Murray
Editor	William Webb
Executive Producers	Paul Bradley
	Osman Eralp
Music	Richard Robbins
Photography	Larry Pizer
Screenplay	Jean-Marie Besset
	George Trow
Producers	Humbert Balsan
	Donald Rosenfeld
Director	Ismail Merchant
Costumes for Jeanne Moreau, Marc Tissot and Christopher Cazenove designed by	Nino Cerruti
Additional Scenes and Dialogue	Andrew Litvack

PARIS

Unit Manager	Nadine Chaussonniere
First Assistant Director	Christopher Granier-Deferre
Second Assistant Director	Nayeem Hafizka
	Alexis Bernier
Sound Recordist	Didier Sain
Boom Operator	Matthieu Imbert
Chief Make-up Artist	Nicolas Degennes
Chief Hairdresser	Fernando Mendes
Make-up Artist	Marie-Luce Fabre-Pajaud
Hairdresser	Ange Pesci
Art Director & Dresser	Bernadette Saint-Loubert
Set Decorator	Patrick Colpaert
Art Department Assistants	Vanessa Flynn
	Frederic Vialle
	Thierry Chavenon
Property Master	Philippe Margottin
Stand-By Prop	Linford Cazenove

211

Assistant Costume Designer	Eric Perron
Wardrobe Mistress	Tina Morel
Wardrobe Assistants	Azmine Jaffer
	Janina Ryba
	Anne Micolod
Follow-Focus Cameraman	Isabelle Ferrandis
Clapper Loader	Claire Caroff
Second Unit Cameraman	Claire Bailly Du Bois
Camera Grip	Angelo Chinosi
Best Boy Grip	Mathieu Ungaro
Grip	Laurent Usse
Gaffer	Michel Gonckel
Best Boy	Michel Vedie
Electrician	Rodolphe Gonckel
Generator Operator	Guy Guermouh
Script Supervisor	Jacqueline Gamard
Script Assistant	Anne Wermelinger
Technical Advisor	Hugues De Laugardier
Assistant to the Director	Melissa Chung
Runner	Sarah Lebas
Production Co-ordinator	Christopher Vann
Location Manager	Jean-Luc Lucas
Assistant to the Producer	Florian Contini
Stills Photographer	Marina Faust
Extras Casting Director	Annette Trumel
Production Accountants	Rahila Bootwala
	Dany Lebigot
Production Assistants	Abel Monem
	Elena Pistorio
	Michel Zemmour
	Pierre Choumeurthe
Unit Drivers	Patricia Van
	Michel Imbert

NEW YORK

Associate Producer	Richard Hawley
Unit Manager	Ian McGloin
First Assistant Director	Steven L. Booth
Second Assistant Director	Michelle Sullivan
Sound Recordist	Larry Loewinger

212

Boom Operator	Tommie Louie
Recordist	Michael Sanchez
Make-up Artist	Tracy Warbin
Hairdresser	Judy Goodman
Set Decorator	C. Ford Wheeler
Art Department Assistant	Gideon Ponte
Stand-by Prop	John Frugal
Dressing Prop	Adrienne Anderson
	Dave Dorenberg
	Willie Roache
Assistant Costume Designer	Barbara Hause
Wardrobe Mistress	Wendy Van Dyke
Wardrobe Assistant	Barbara Krathauer
1st Assistant Cameraman	Bill Gerardo
2nd Assistant Cameraman	Joe Volpe
Video Technicians	Brian Carmichael
	Dennis Green
Key Grip	Tim Smythe
Best Boy	Anthony Ciotti
Grips	John Gabrielle
	James McMillan
	Michael Eric Slifkin
Gaffer	Scott Ramsey
Best Boy	Mark Schwetner
Electrician	Michael Fradianni
Generator Operator	Rocco Palmieri
Script Supervisor	Christine Gee
Assistant to the Director	Melissa Chung
Production Co-ordinator	Judith Schell
Assistant to the Producer	Carolina Herrera
Stills Photographer	Seth Rubin
Production Accountant	Sunil Kirparam
Assistant Accountant	Alex Mera
Location Manager	Joe Stephans
Locations Assistant	Rozi Jovanovic
Parking Co-ordinator	Leon Adair
Production Assistants	Aldo Romero
	Raphael Osorio
	Dave Lampher
	Dove Greenberg

213

	Michael Albanese
	Darin Kevin
	Darin Tellinger
	Timothy Hollis
Runners	Anne Field
	Evan Friel
	Carol Burton
	Melanie Simpson
Teamster Captain	Jim Nugent
Teamster Drivers	Daniel Palmer
	Kevin Fennigan

LONDON

Editorial Consultant	Humphrey Dixon
Assistant Editor	Anne K. Aylward
Apprentice Editor	Dmitri Vigneswaren
	Claire Ferguson
Supervising Sound Editor	Alexander Campbell Askew
Dialogue Editor	Robert Gavin
Foley Editor	William Trent
Assistant Sound Editor	Derek Lomas
	Laura Evans
Sound Re-recording Mixer	John Hayward
Production Co-ordinator	Sian Parry
Production Assistants	Sarah Strupinski
	Andrew Haigh
Orchestral Arranger	Geoffrey Alexander
Music Conductor	Harry Rabinowitz
Music Recording Engineer	Bill Somerville-Large
Music Copyist	Matt Dunkley